ANOTHER LOOK
PORTRAITS IN CARICATURE

Copyright © 2018 John Champlin.
All rights reserved.

"Who sees the human face correctly:
the photographer, the mirror, or the painter?"

-Pablo Picasso

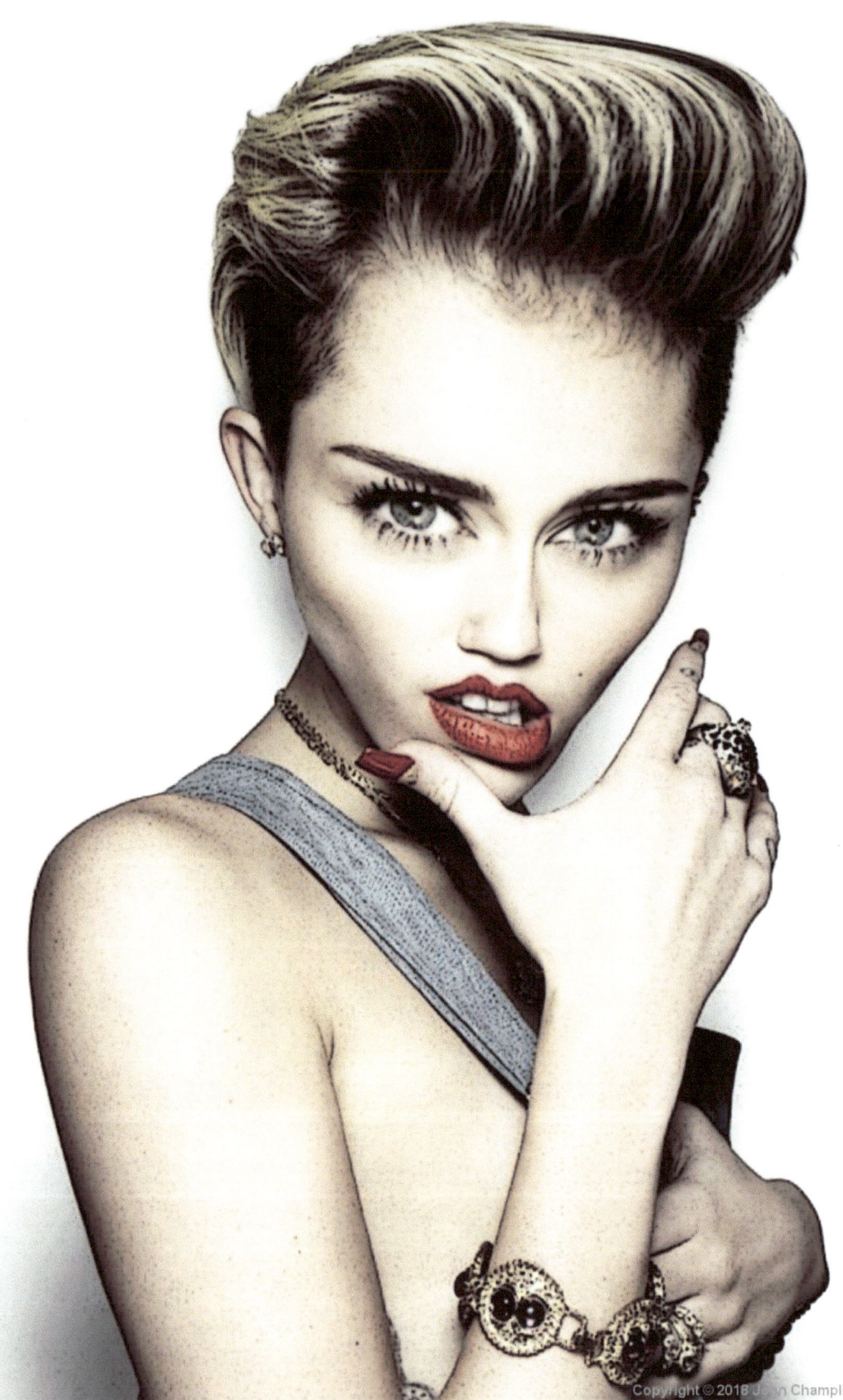

Miley Cyrus

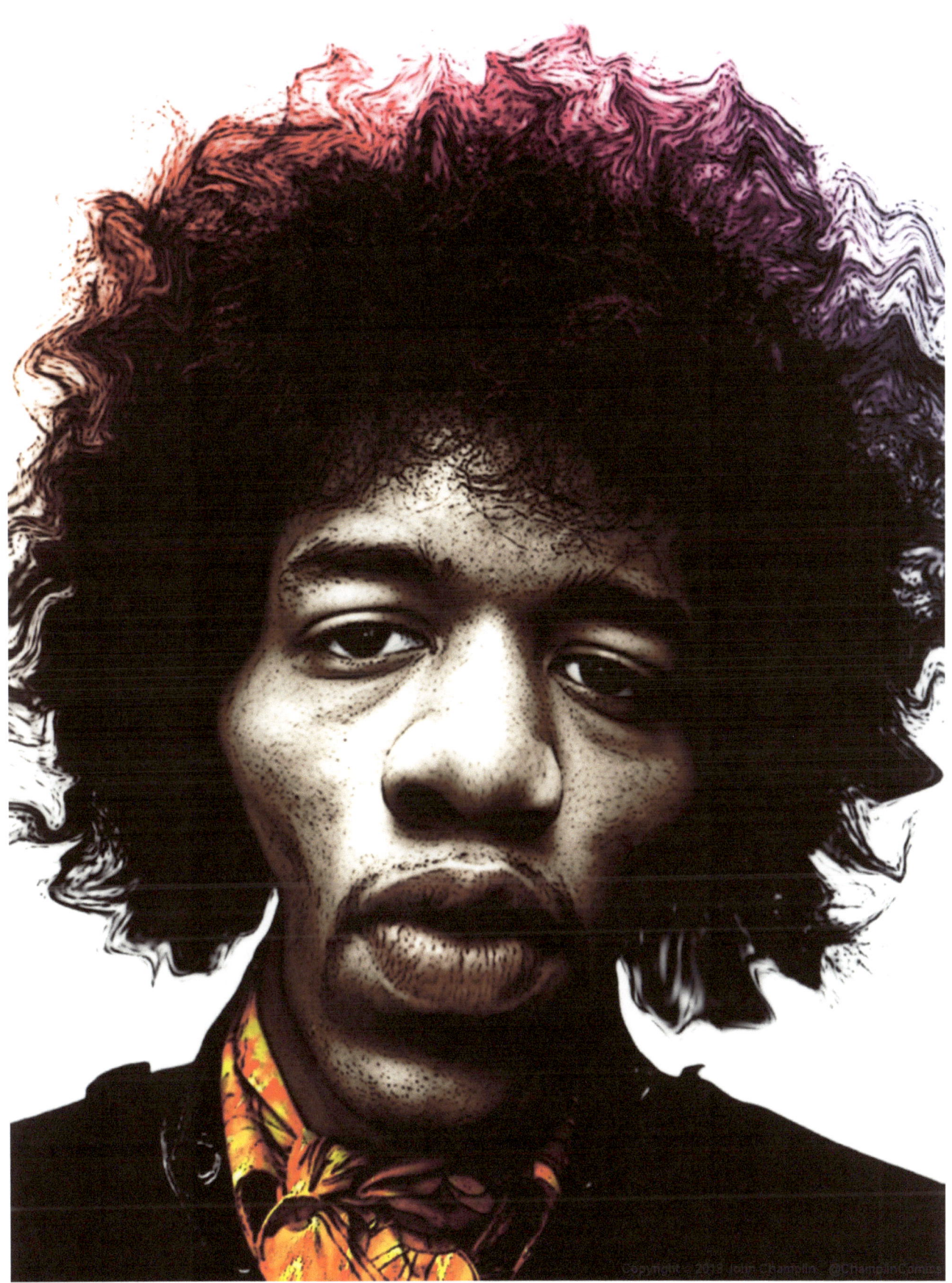

Jimi Hendrix

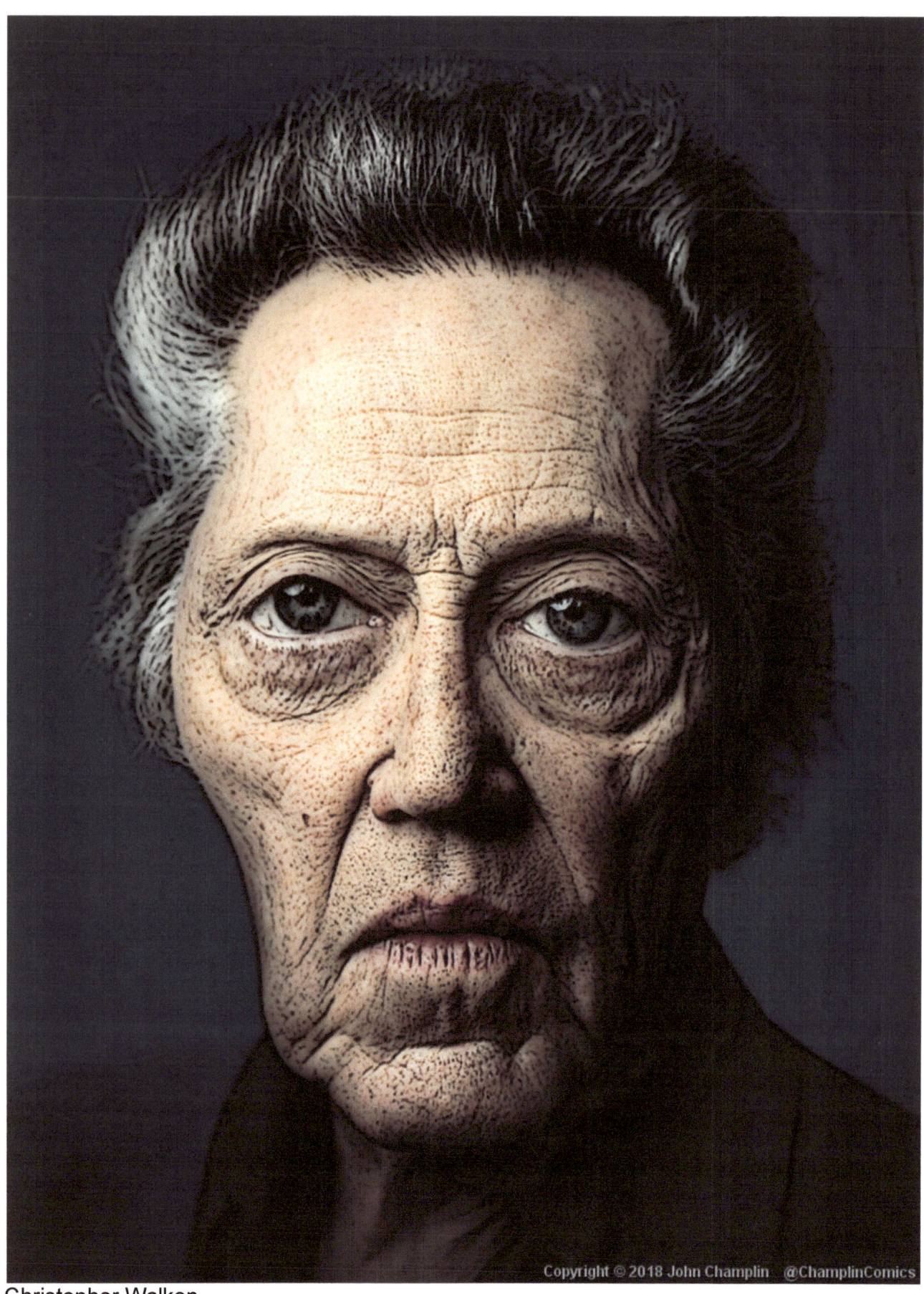

Christopher Walken

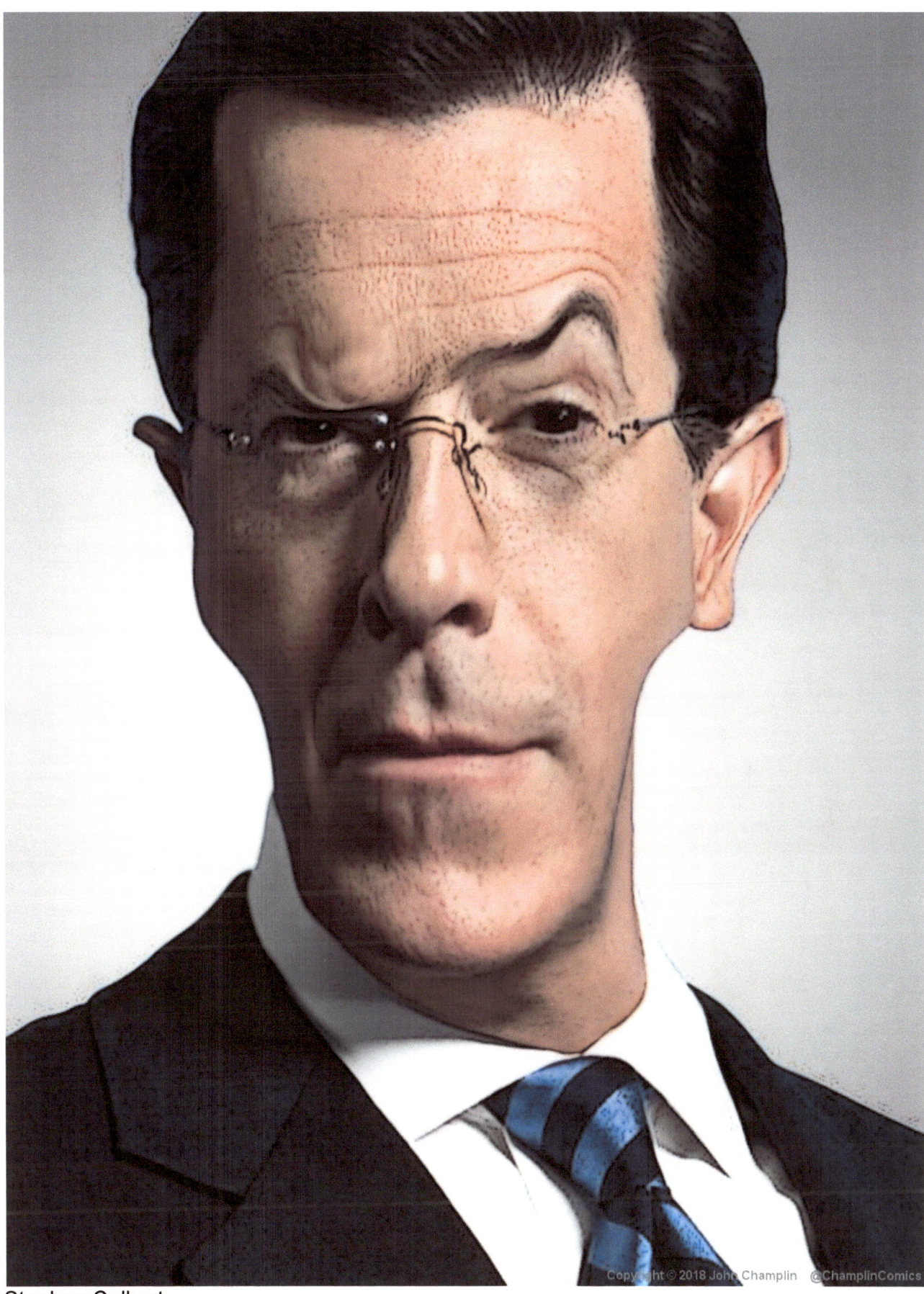

Stephen Colbert

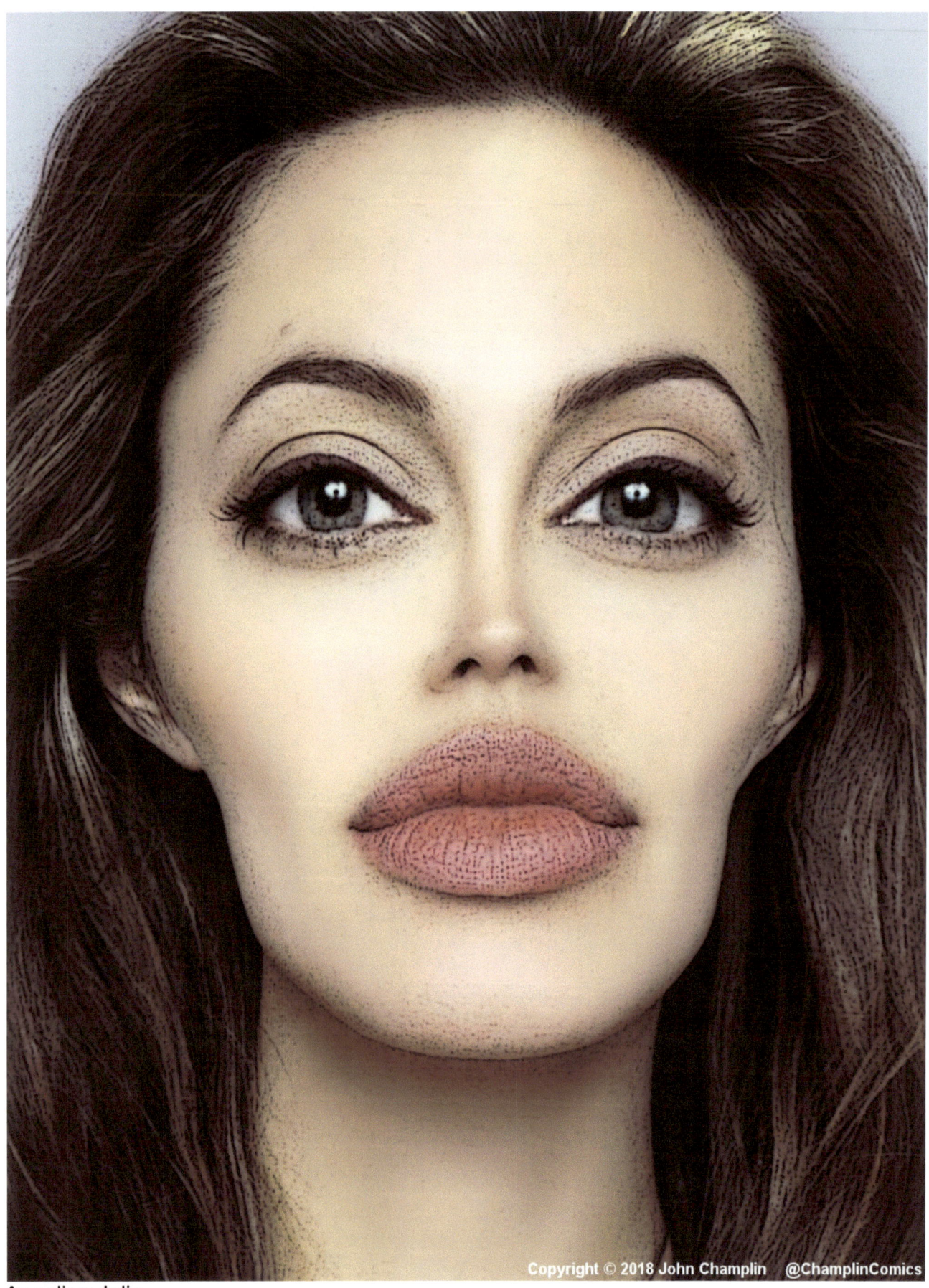

Angelina Jolie

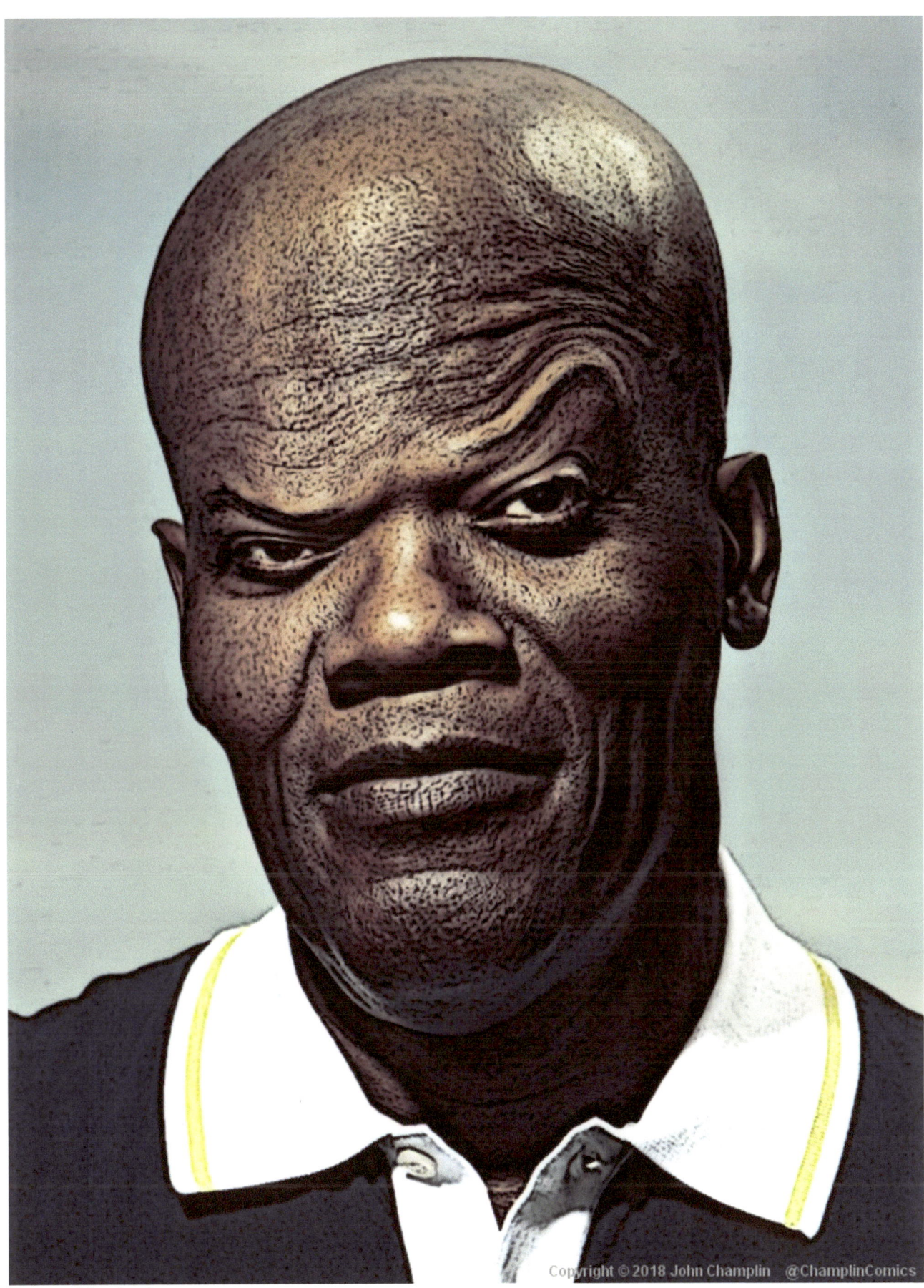

Samuel L. Jackson

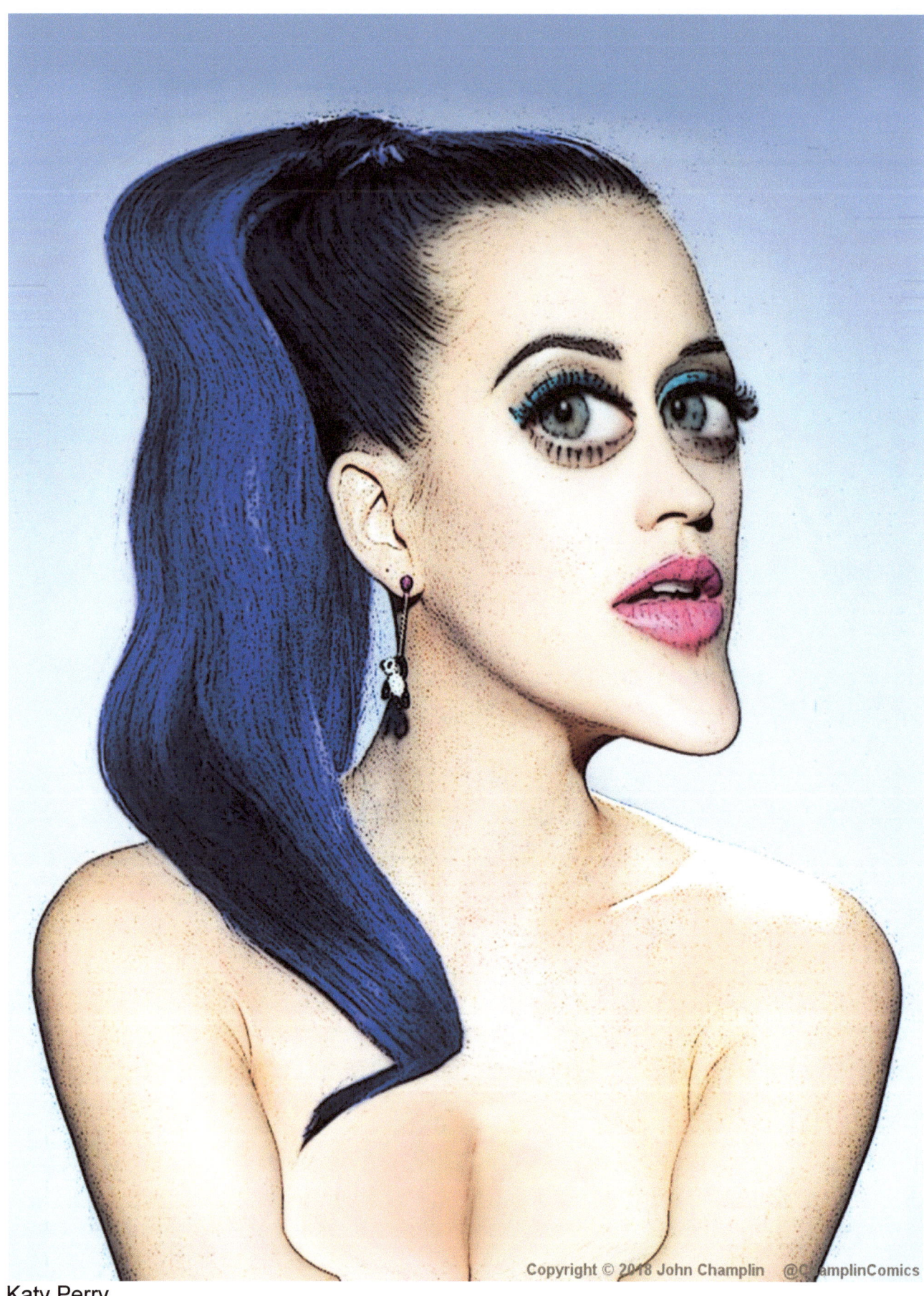

Katy Perry

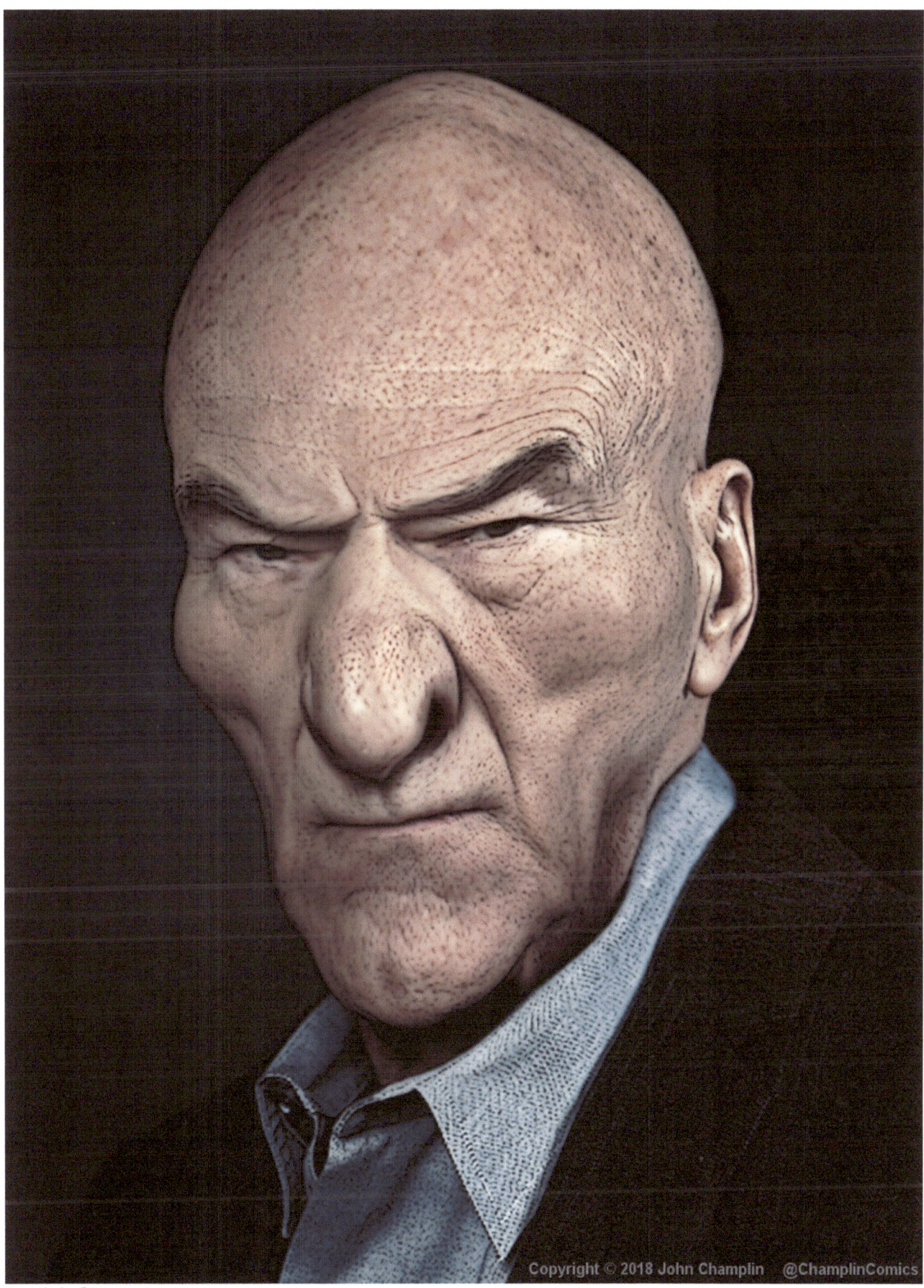

Patrick Stewart

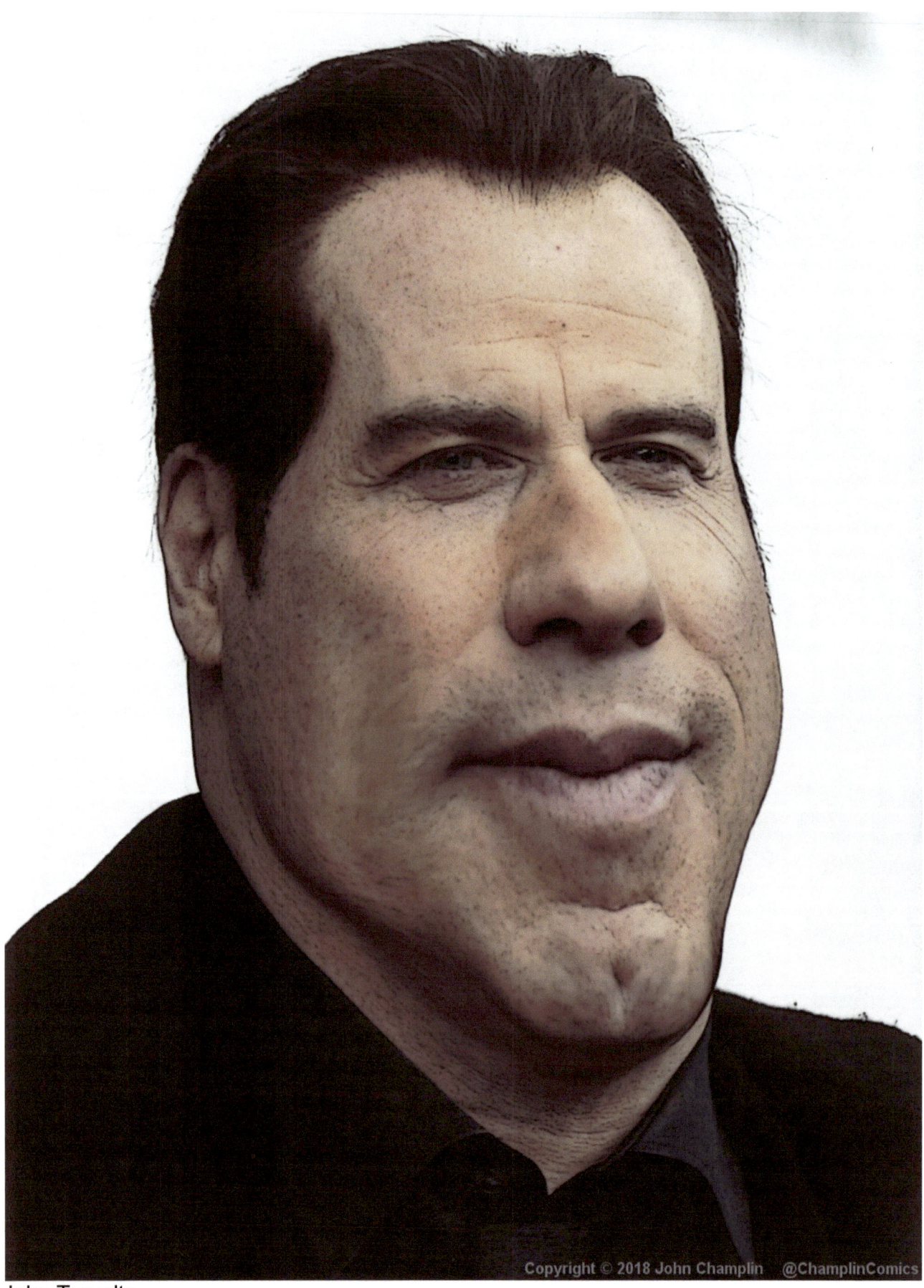

John Travolta

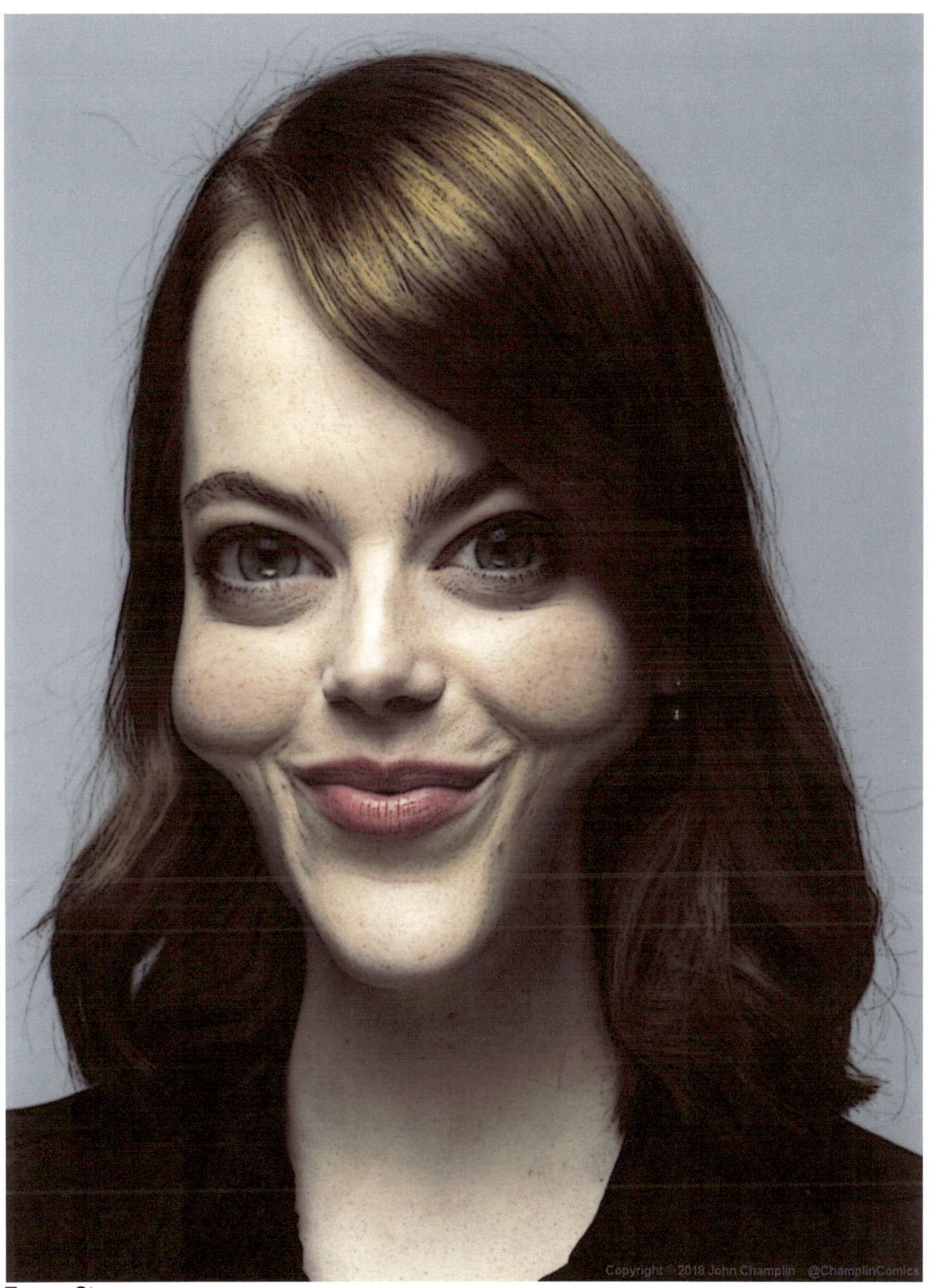

Emma Stone

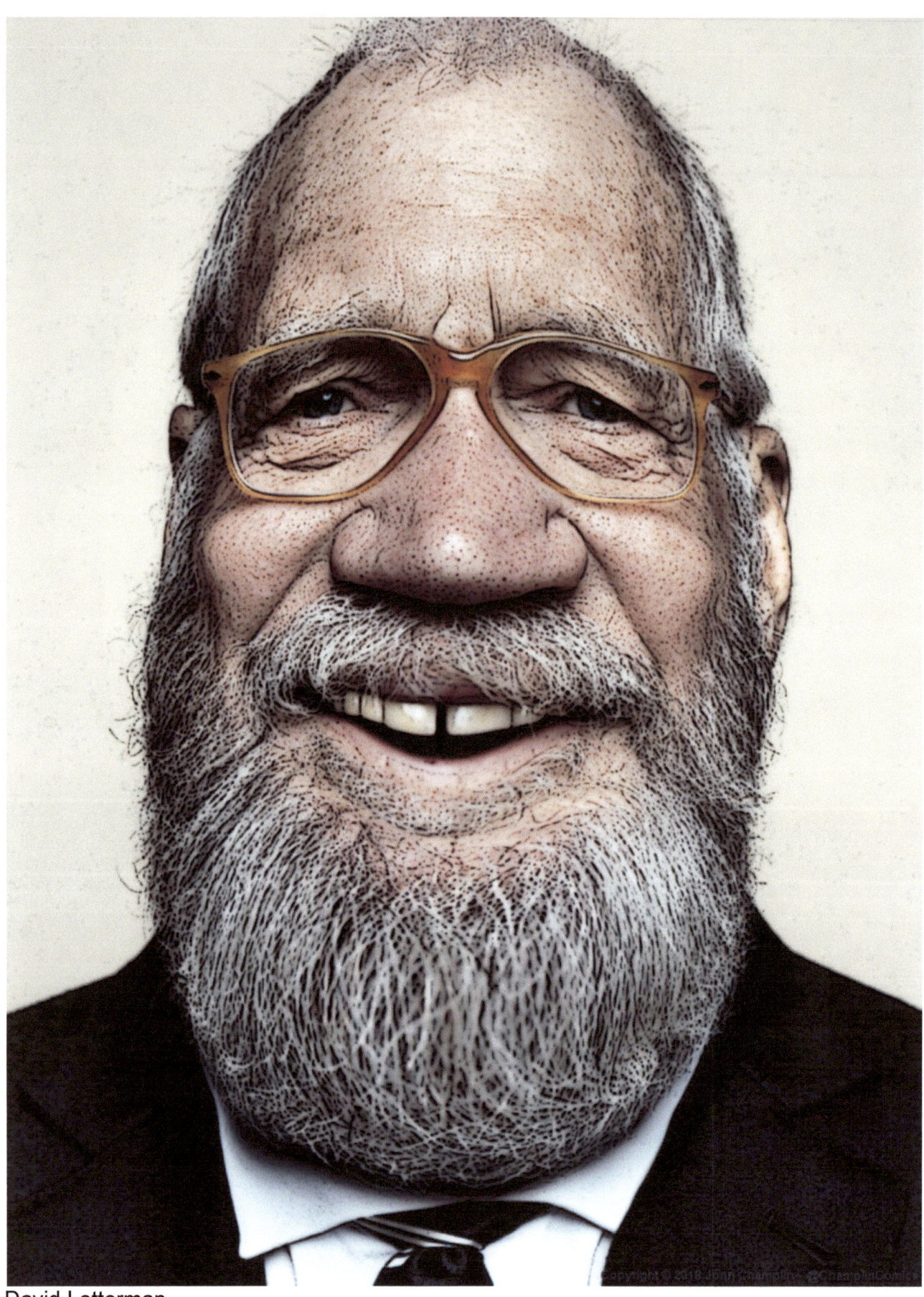

David Letterman

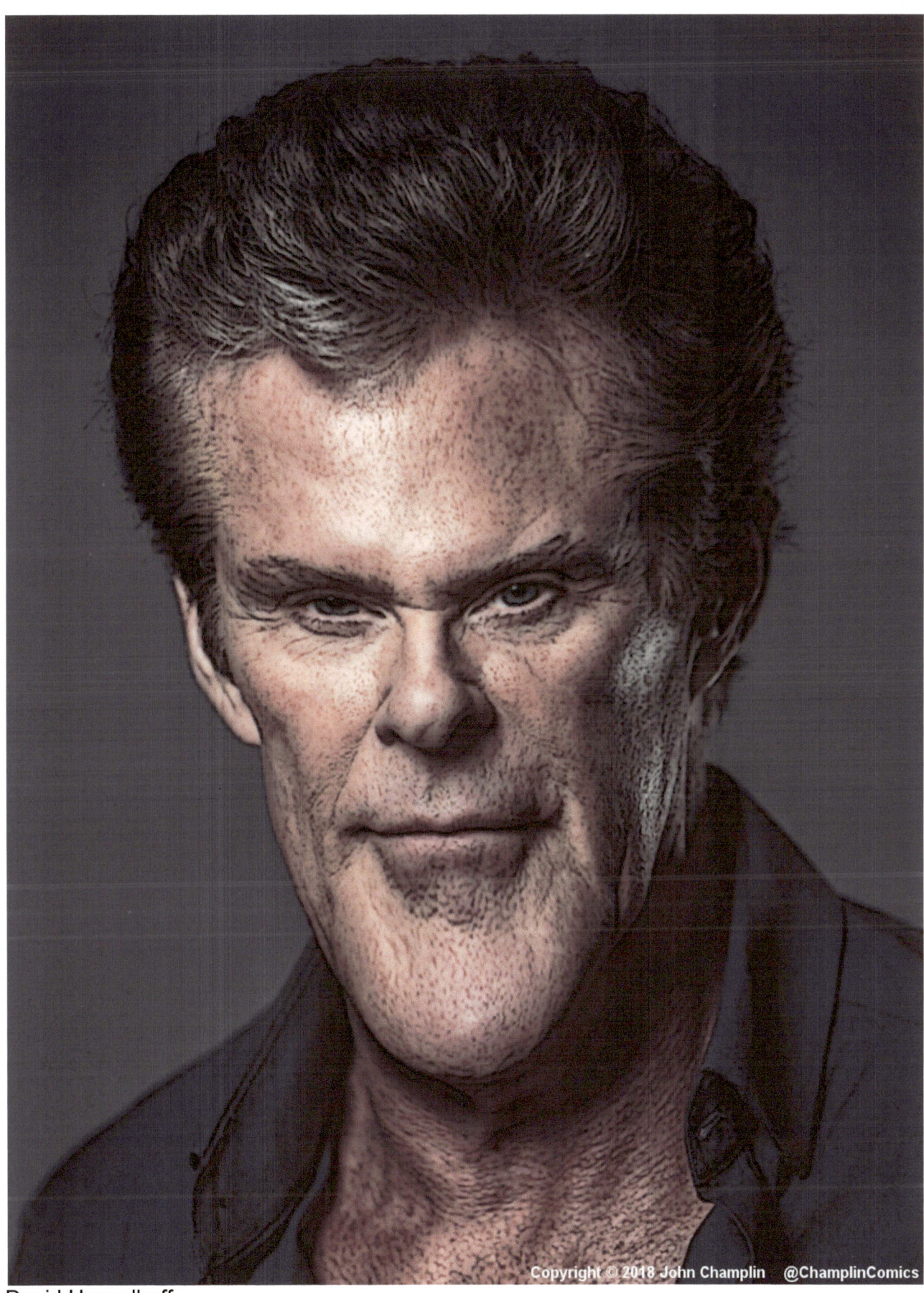

David Hasselhoff

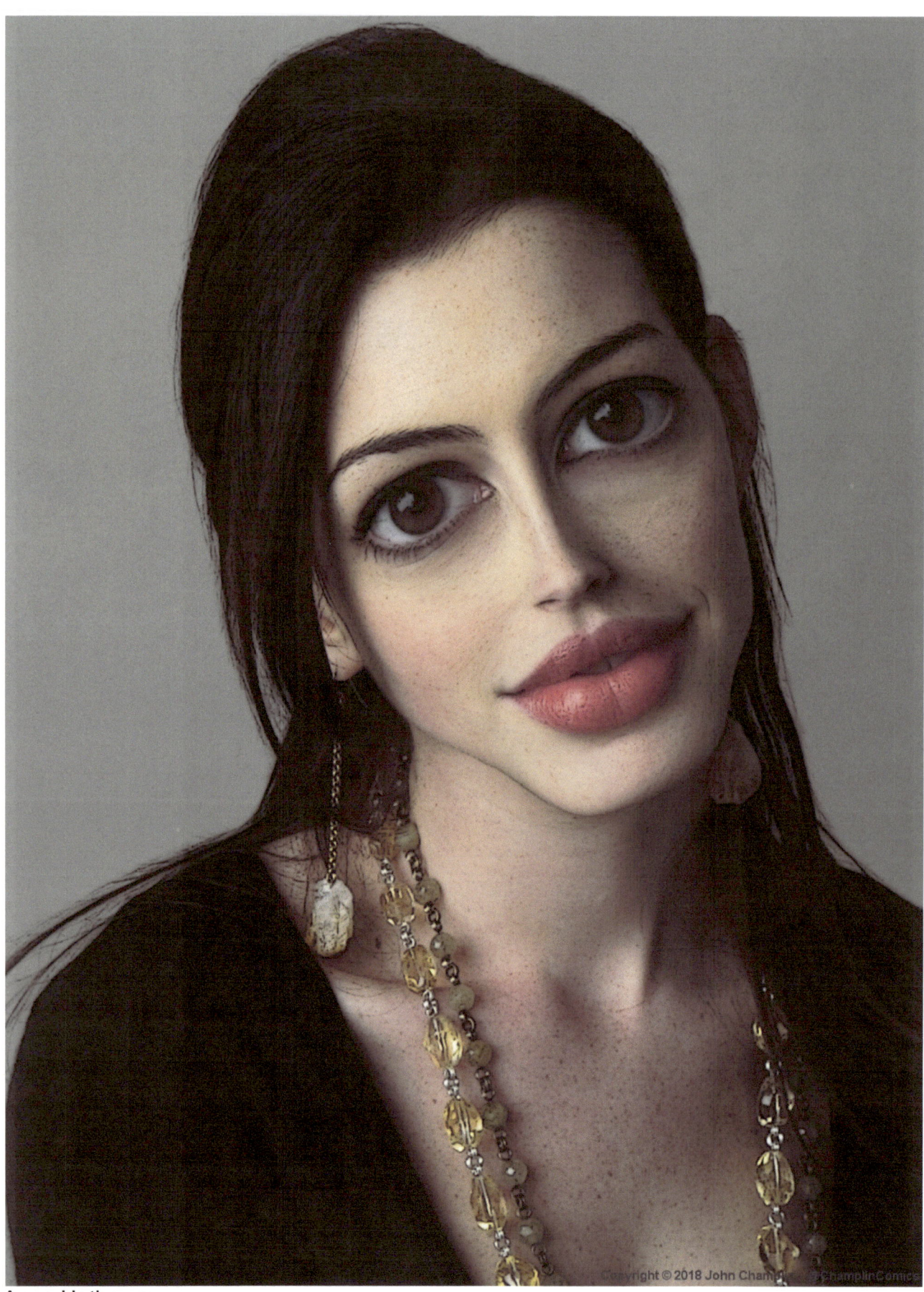

Anne Hathaway

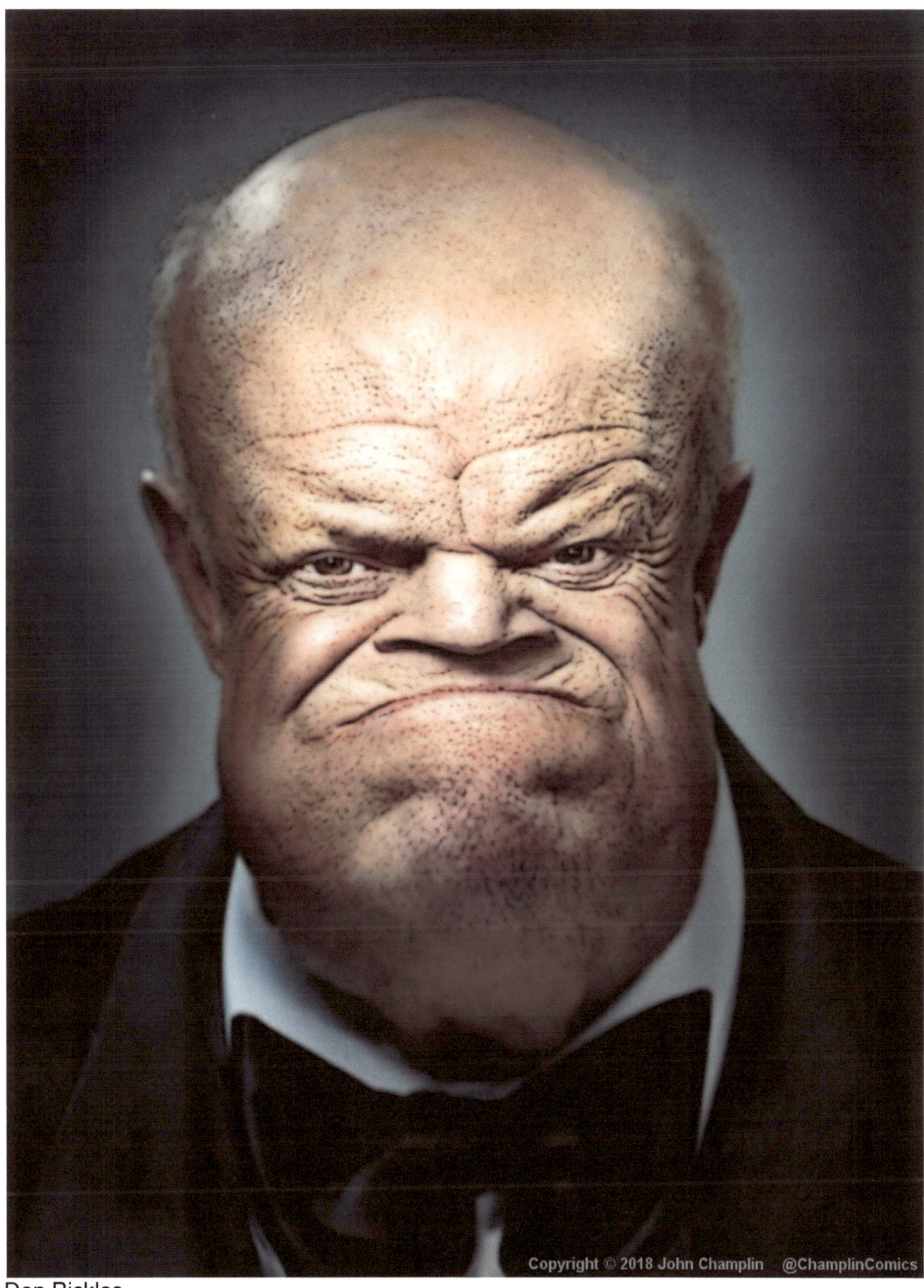

Don Rickles

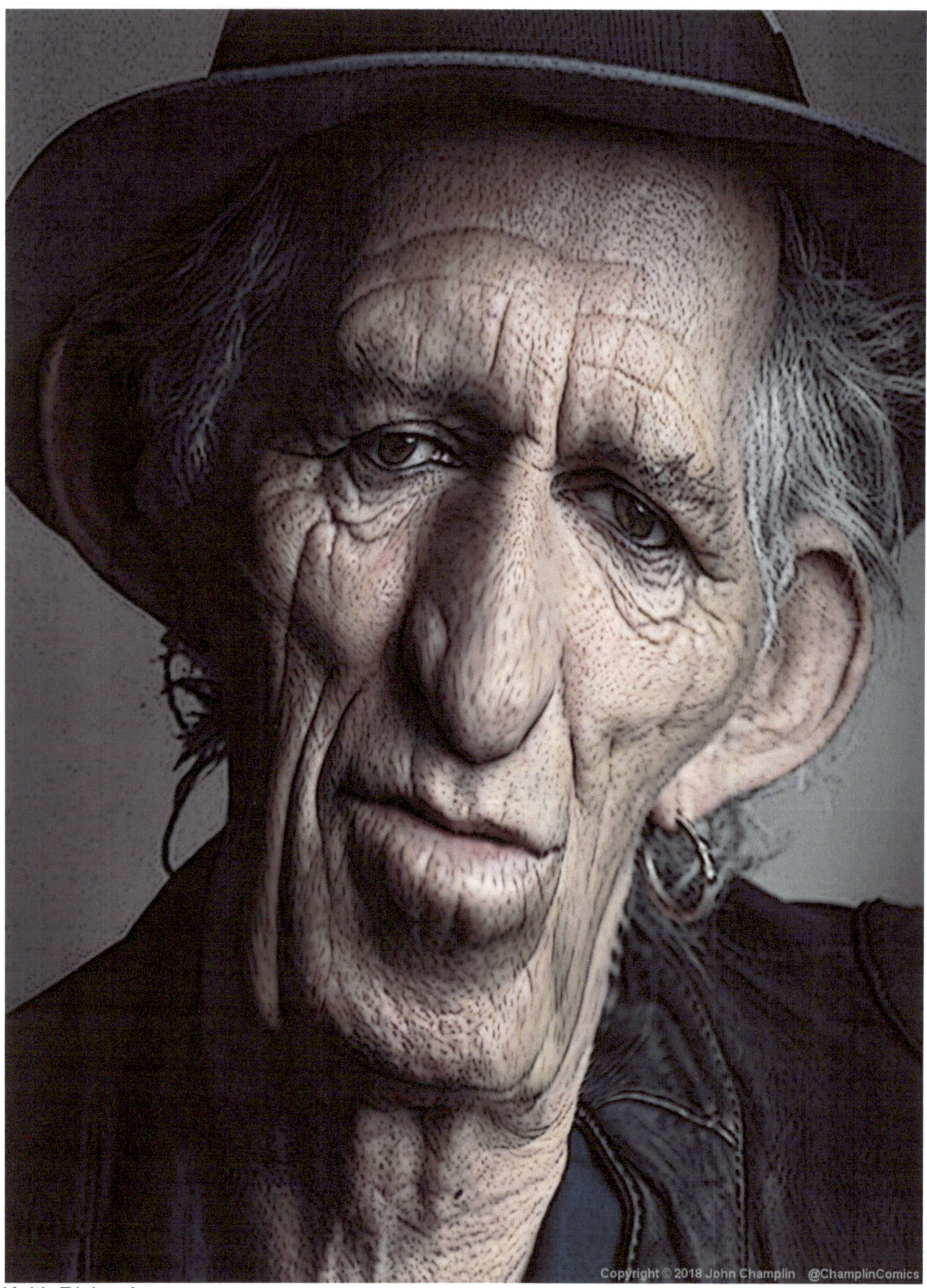

Keith Richards

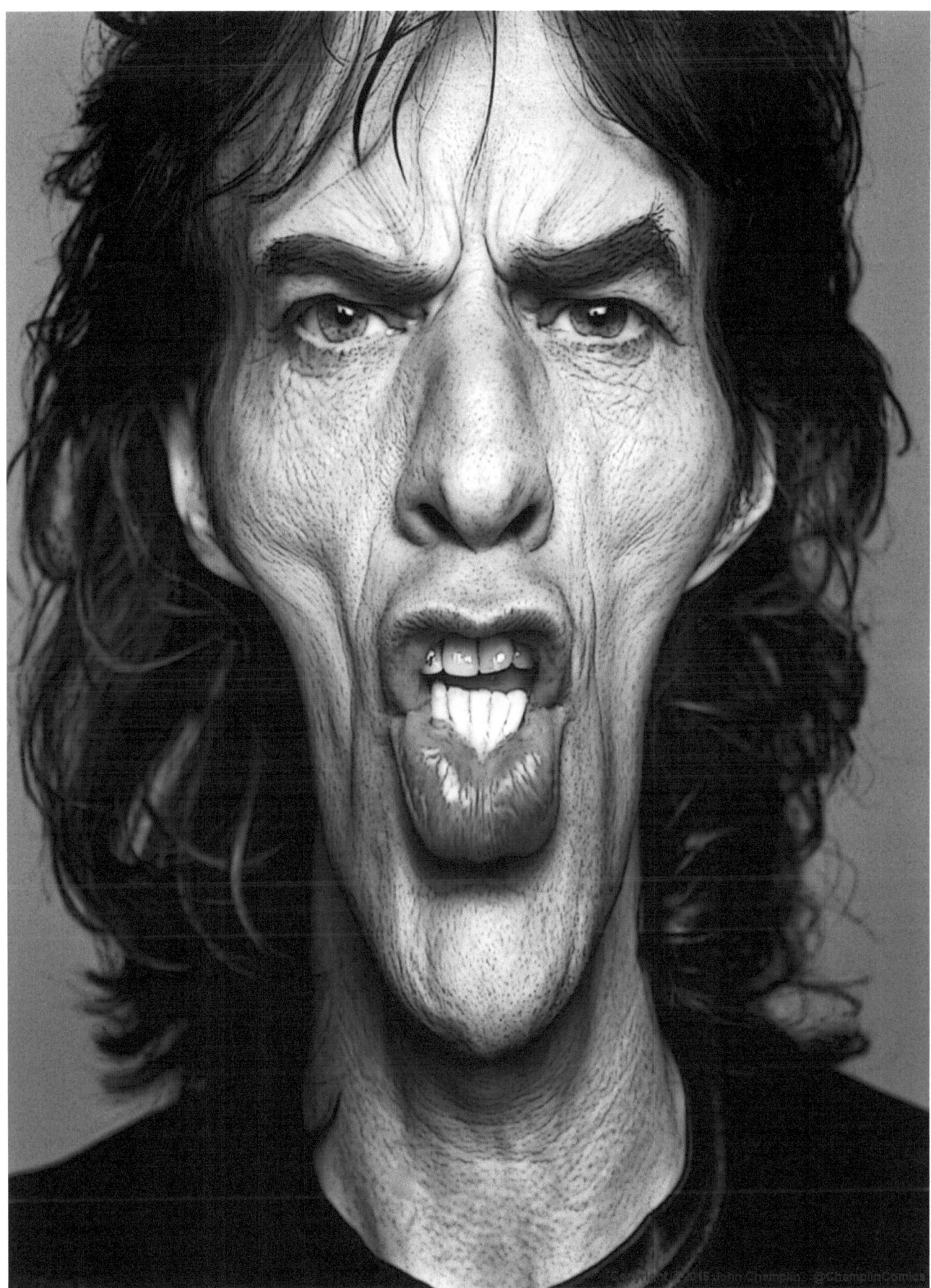

Mick Jagger

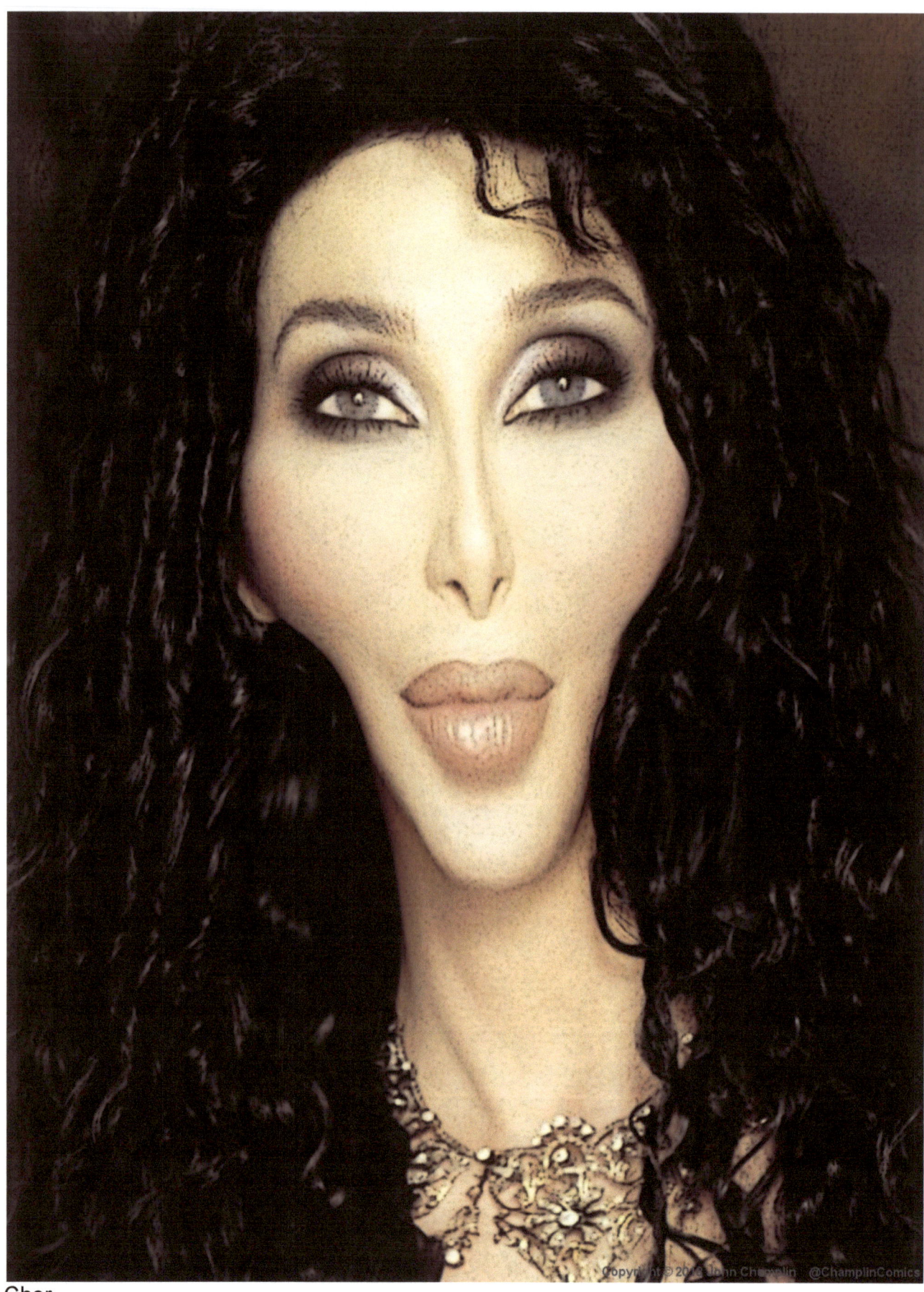

Cher

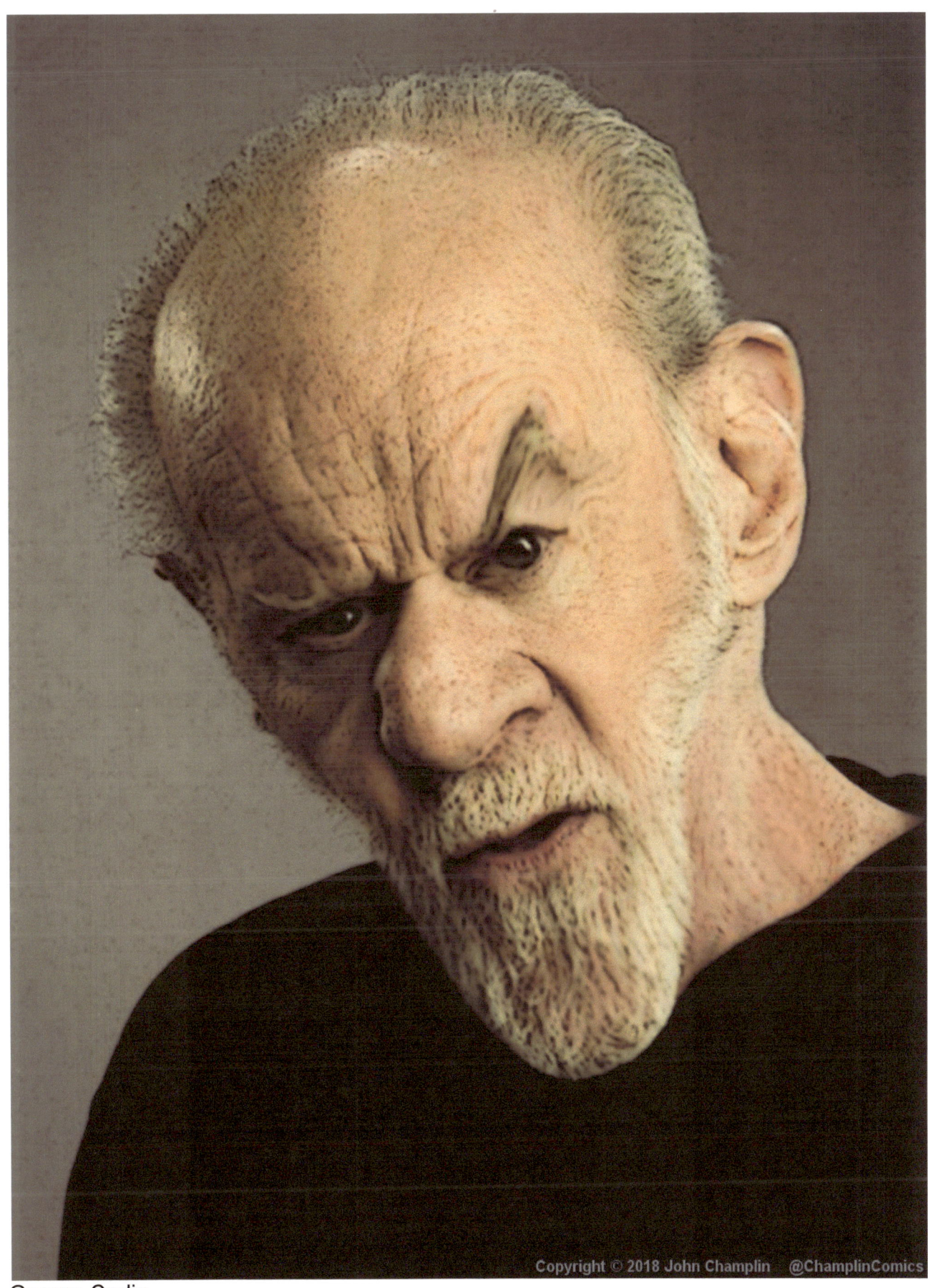

George Carlin

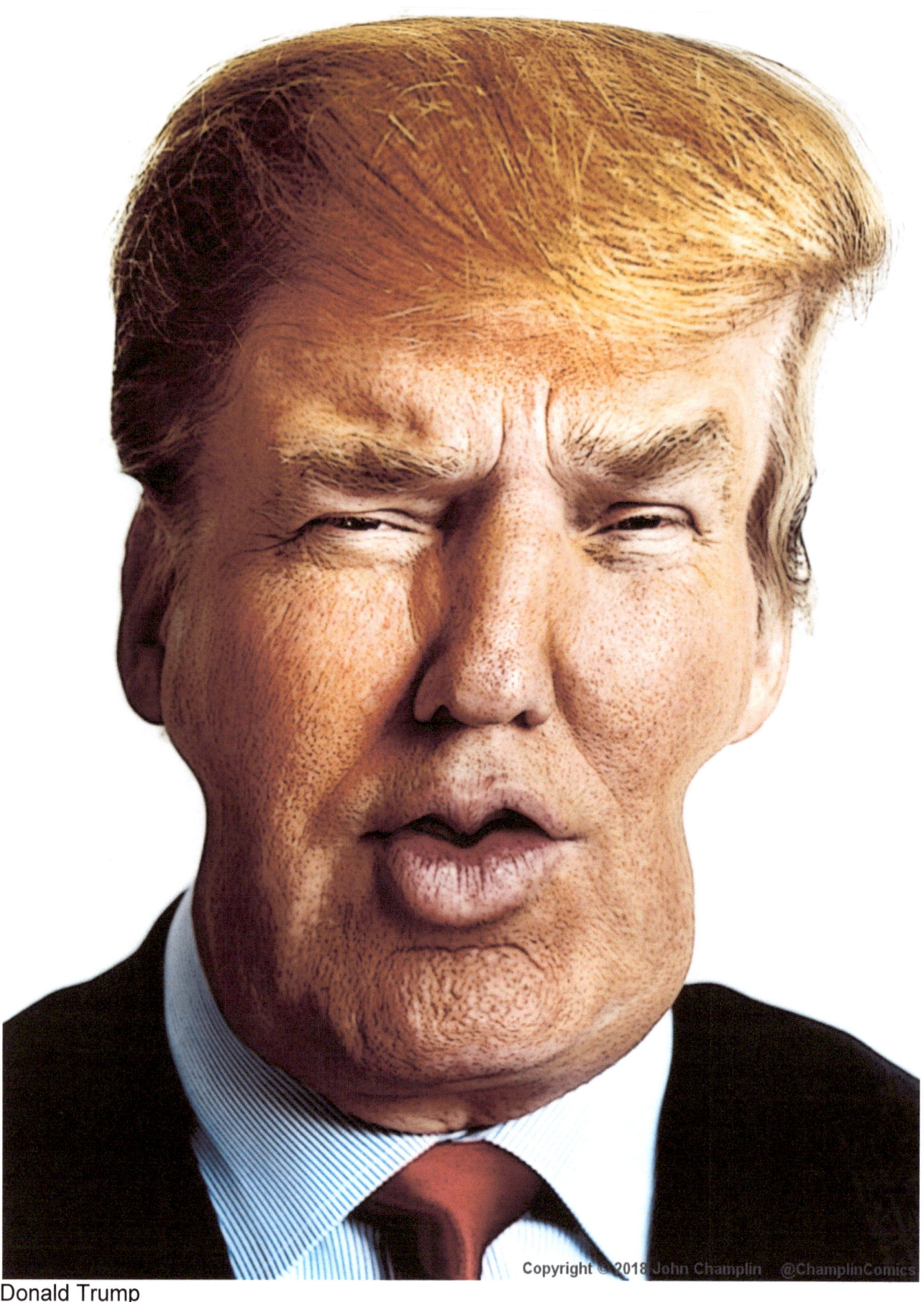

Donald Trump

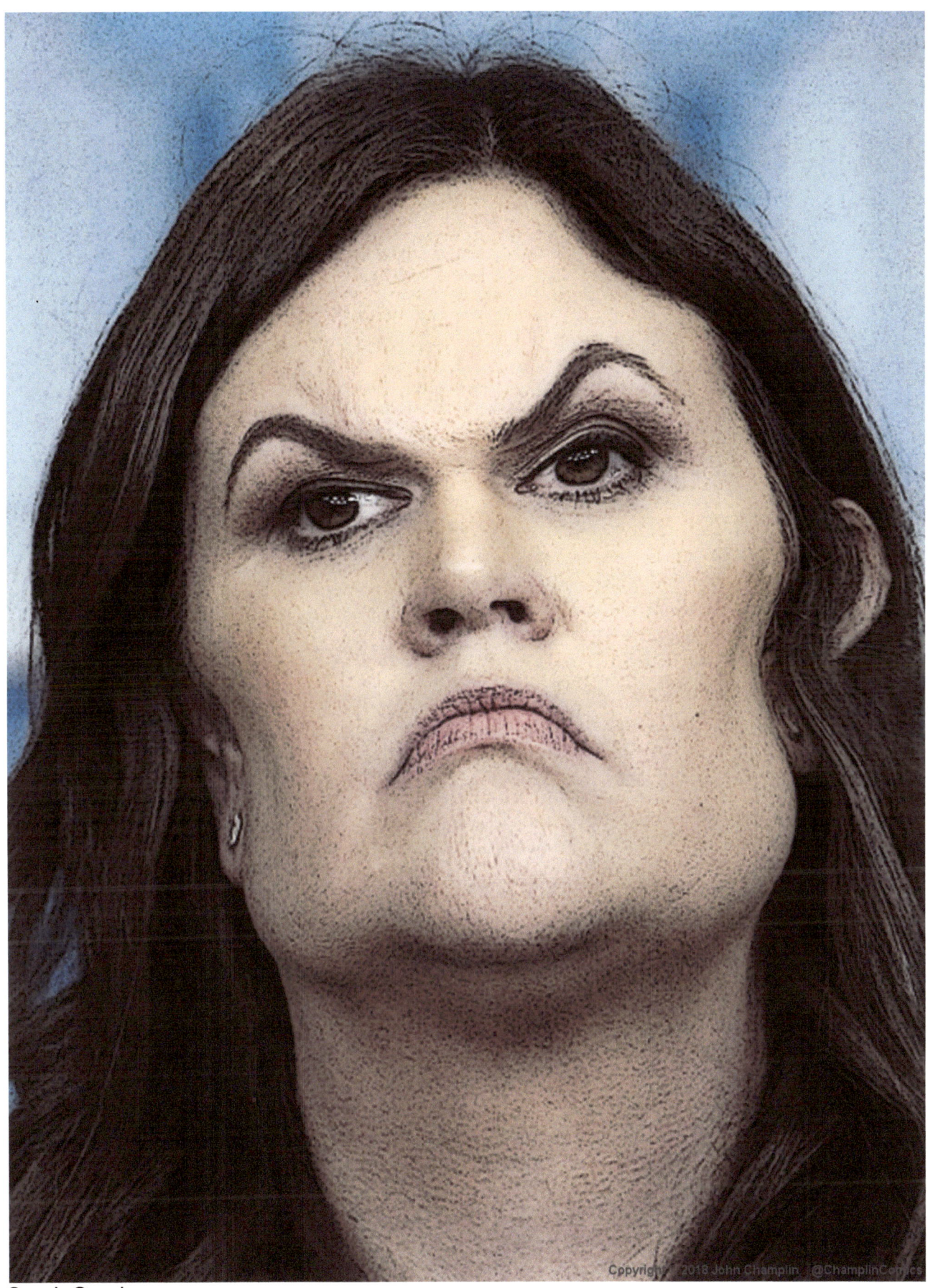

Sarah Sanders

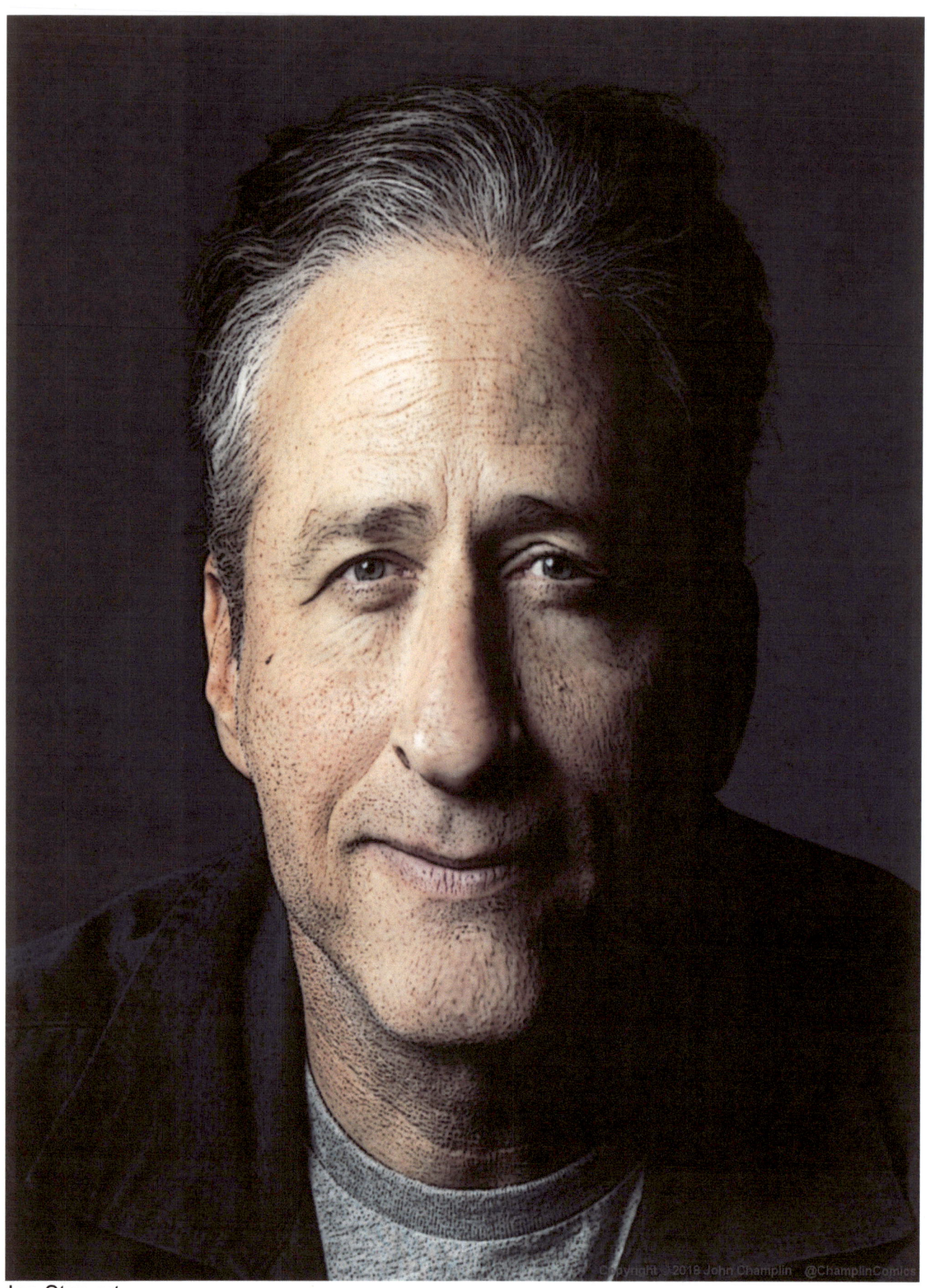

Jon Stewart

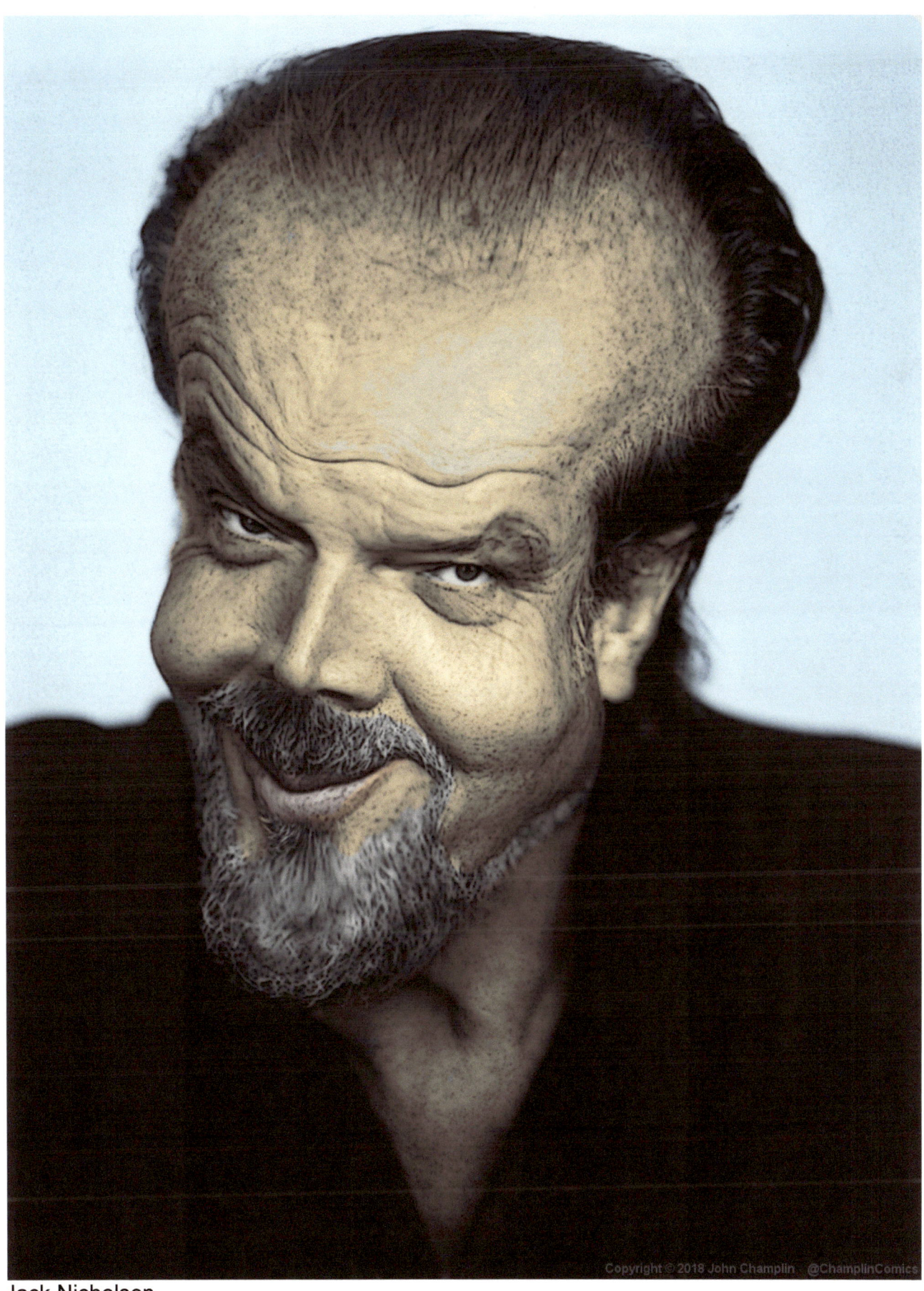

Jack Nicholson

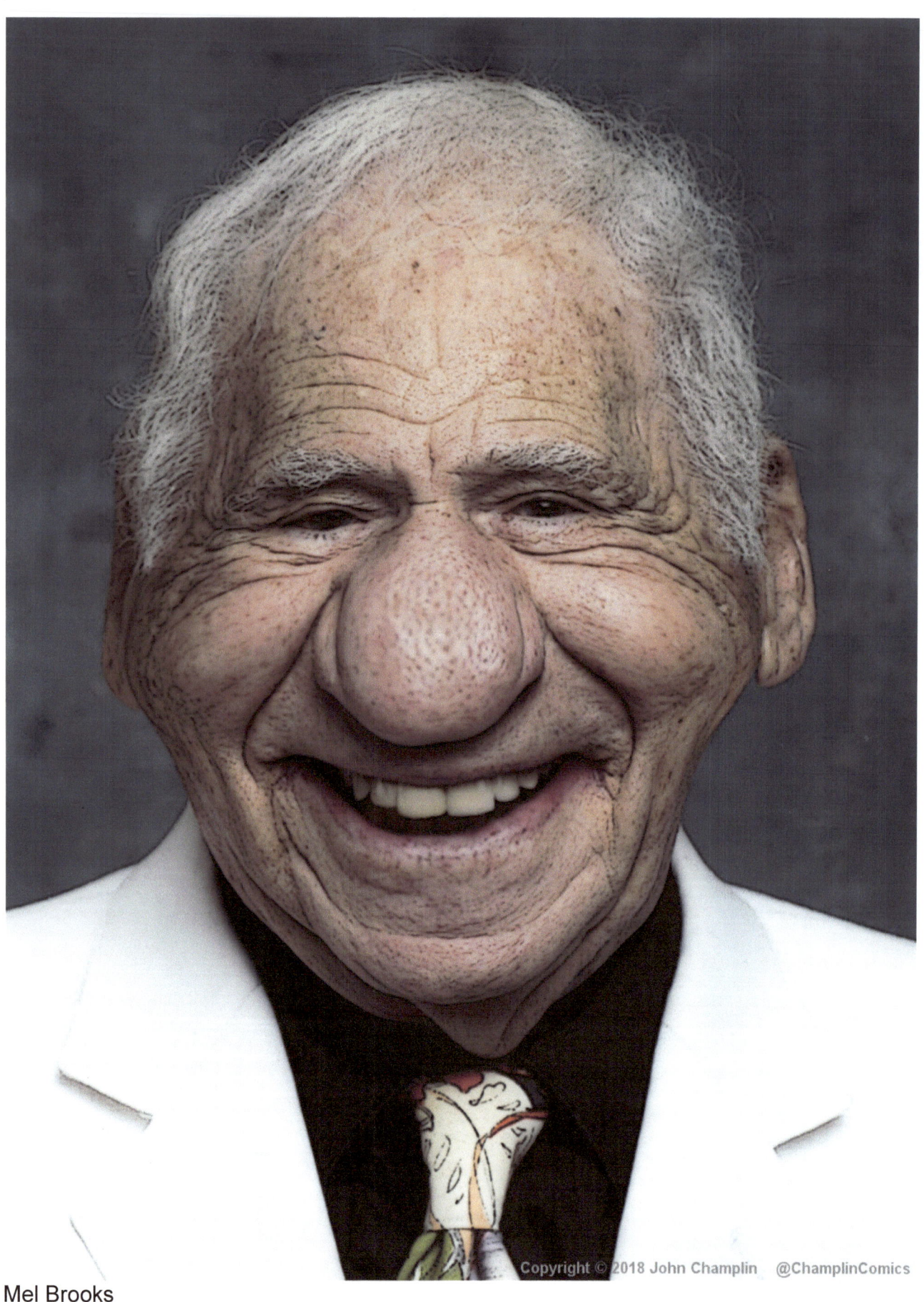

Mel Brooks

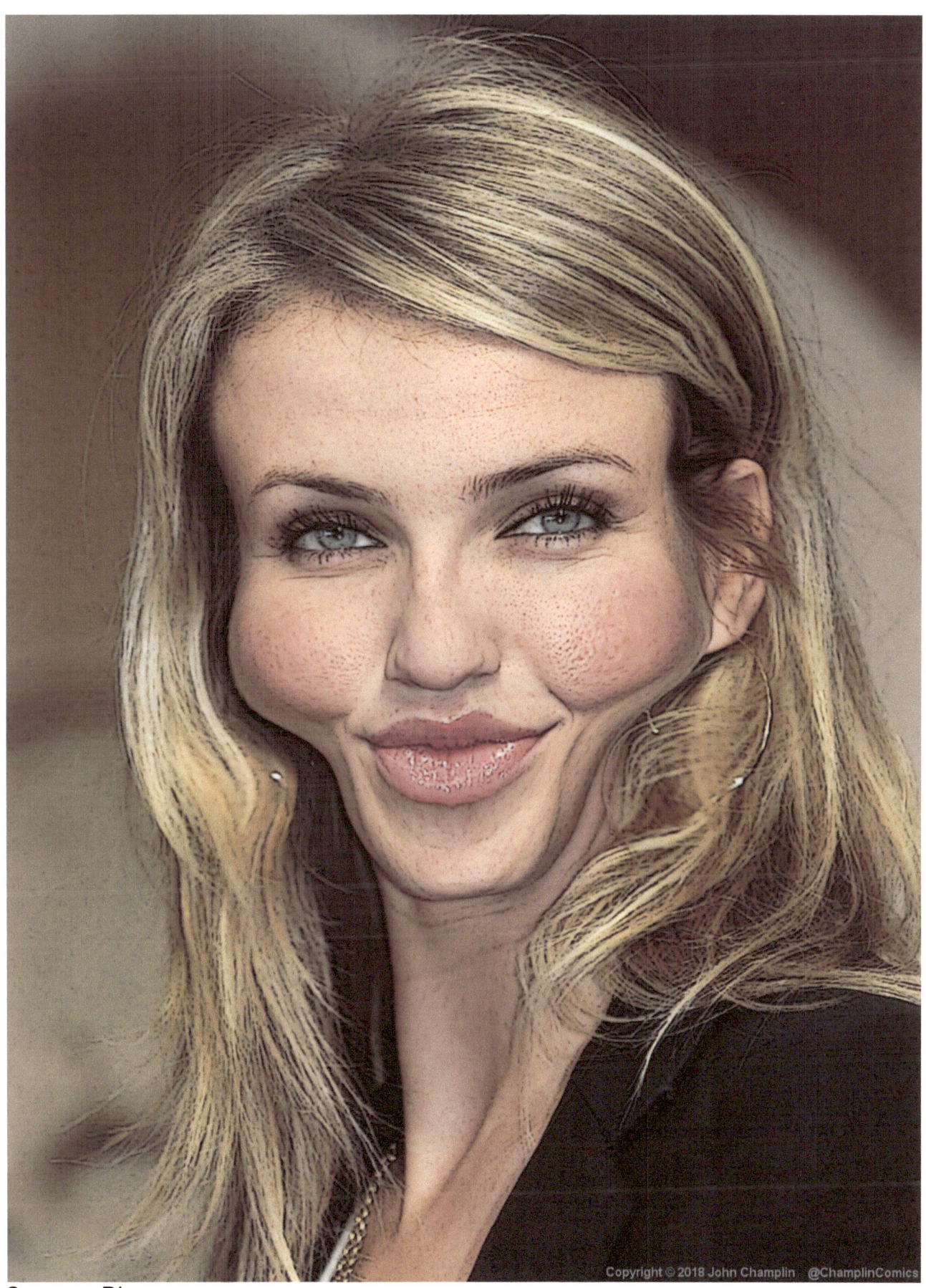

Cameron Diaz

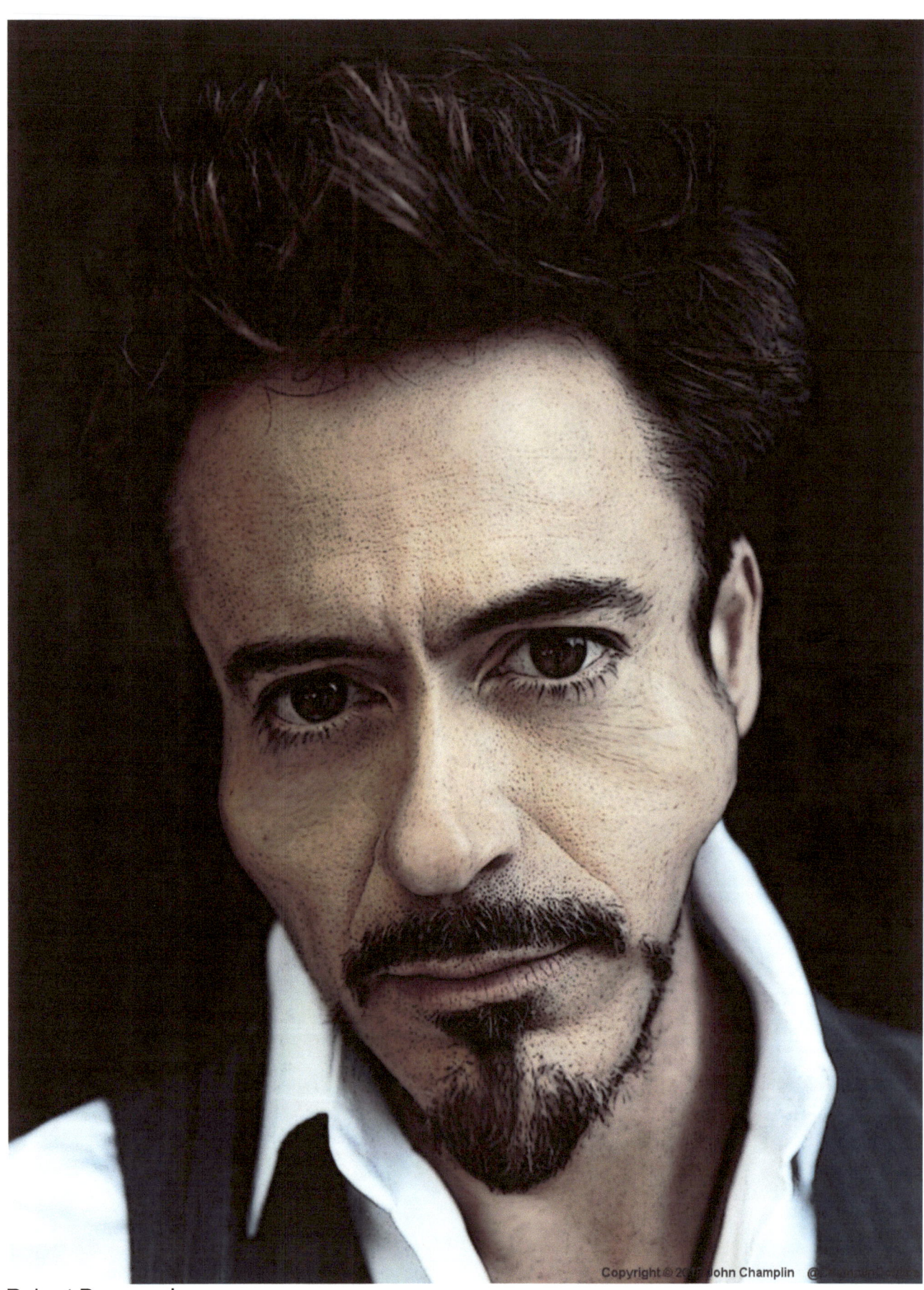

Robert Downey Jr.

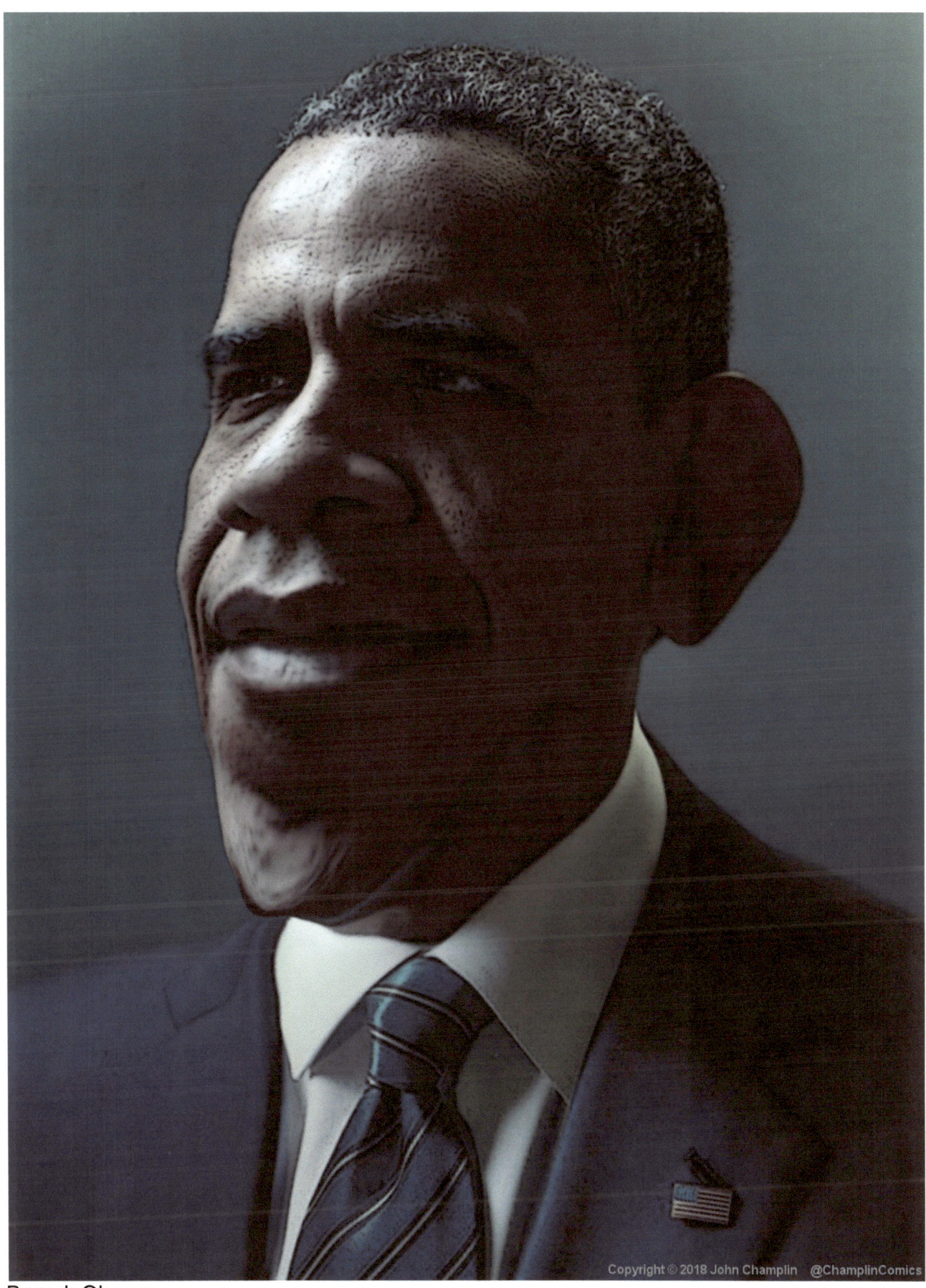

Barack Obama

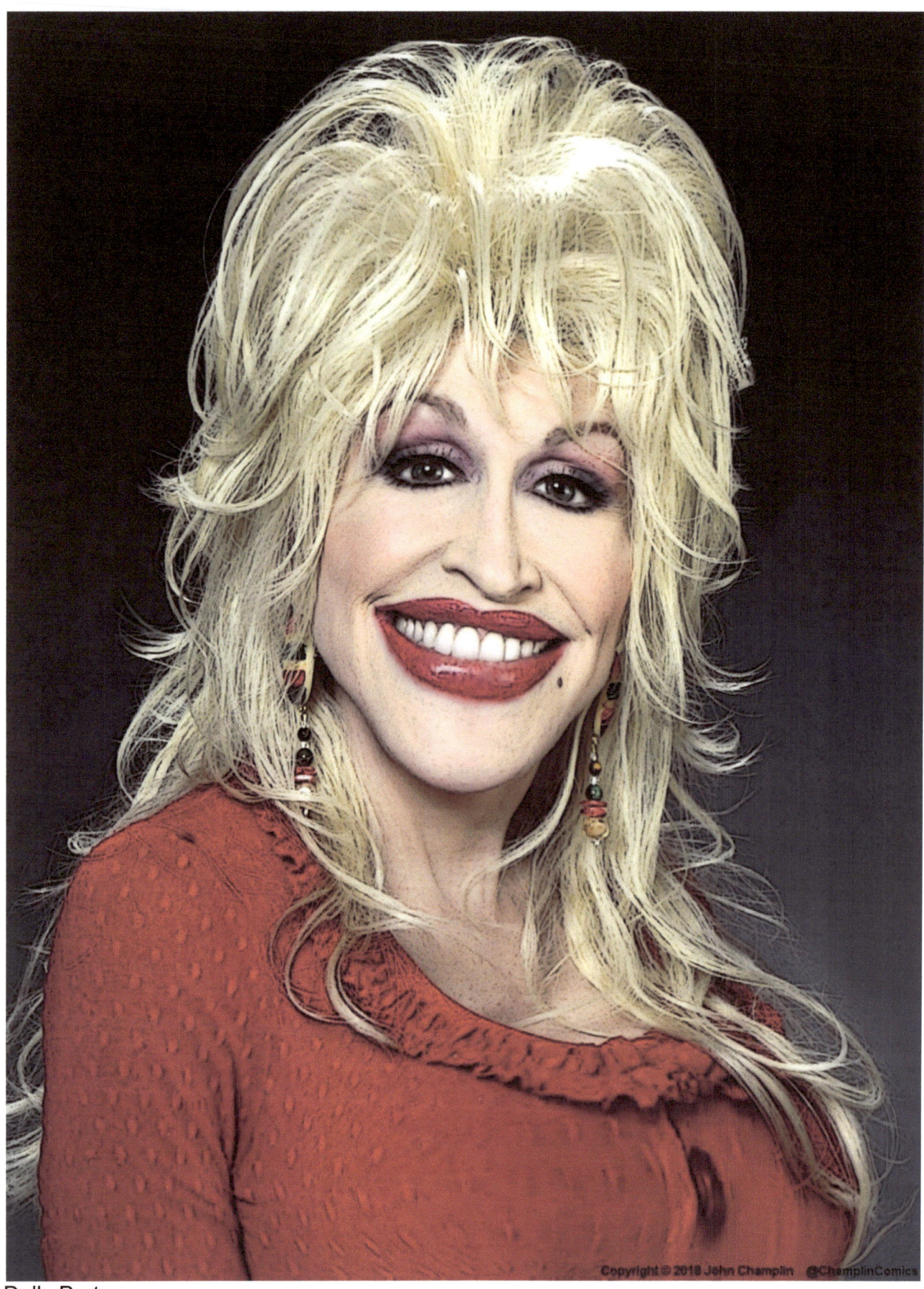

Dolly Parton

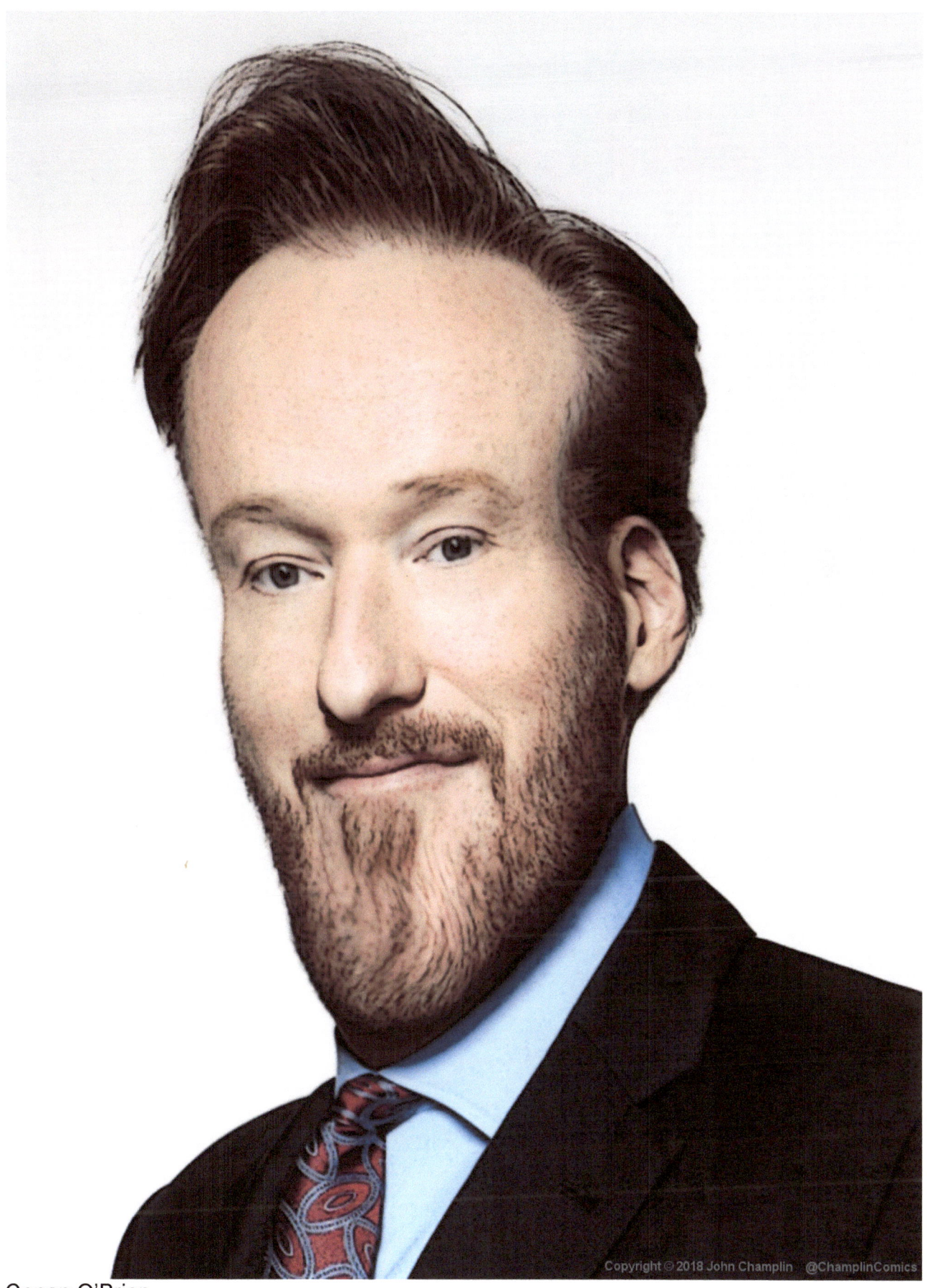

Conan O'Brien

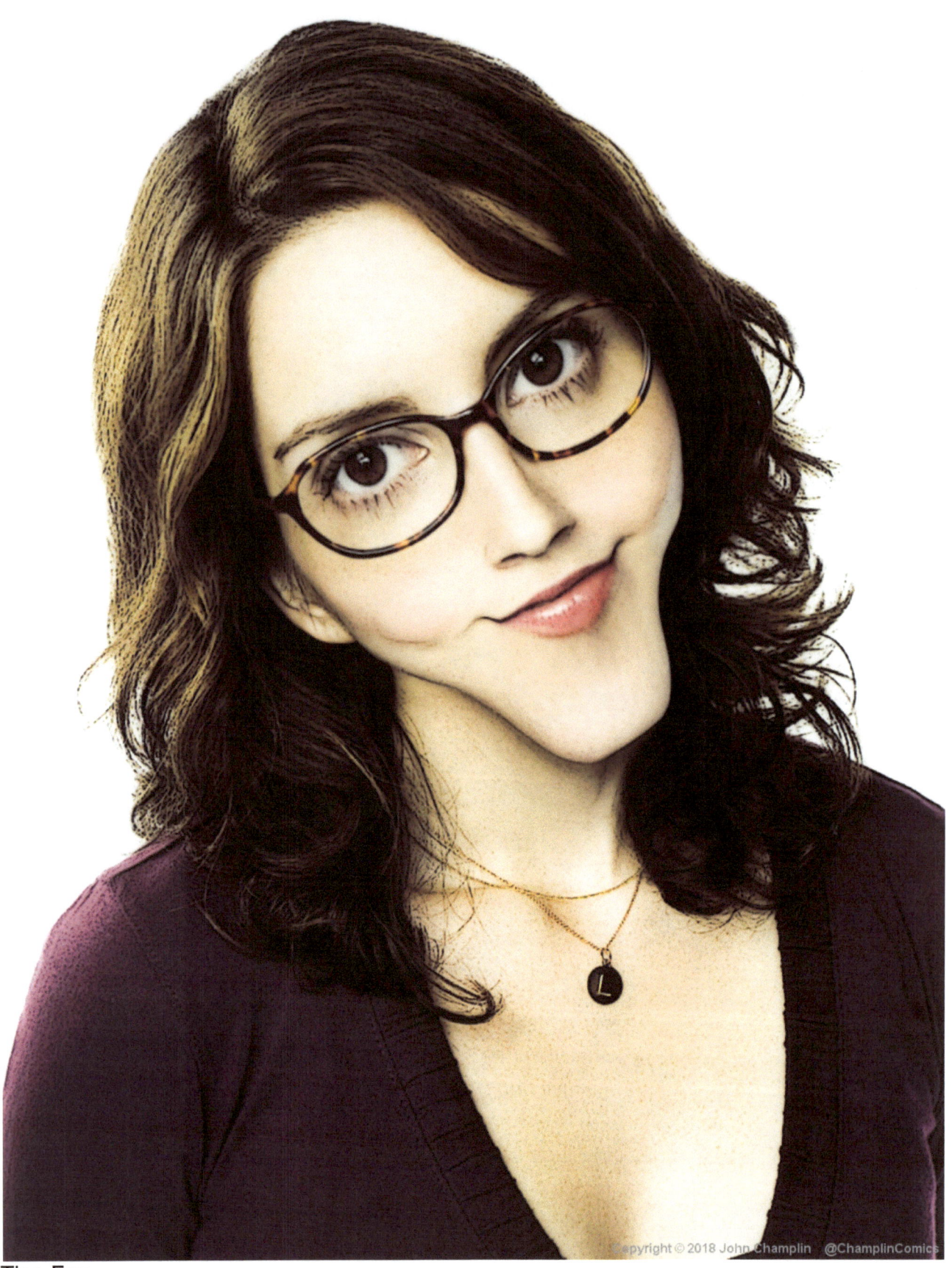

Tina Fey

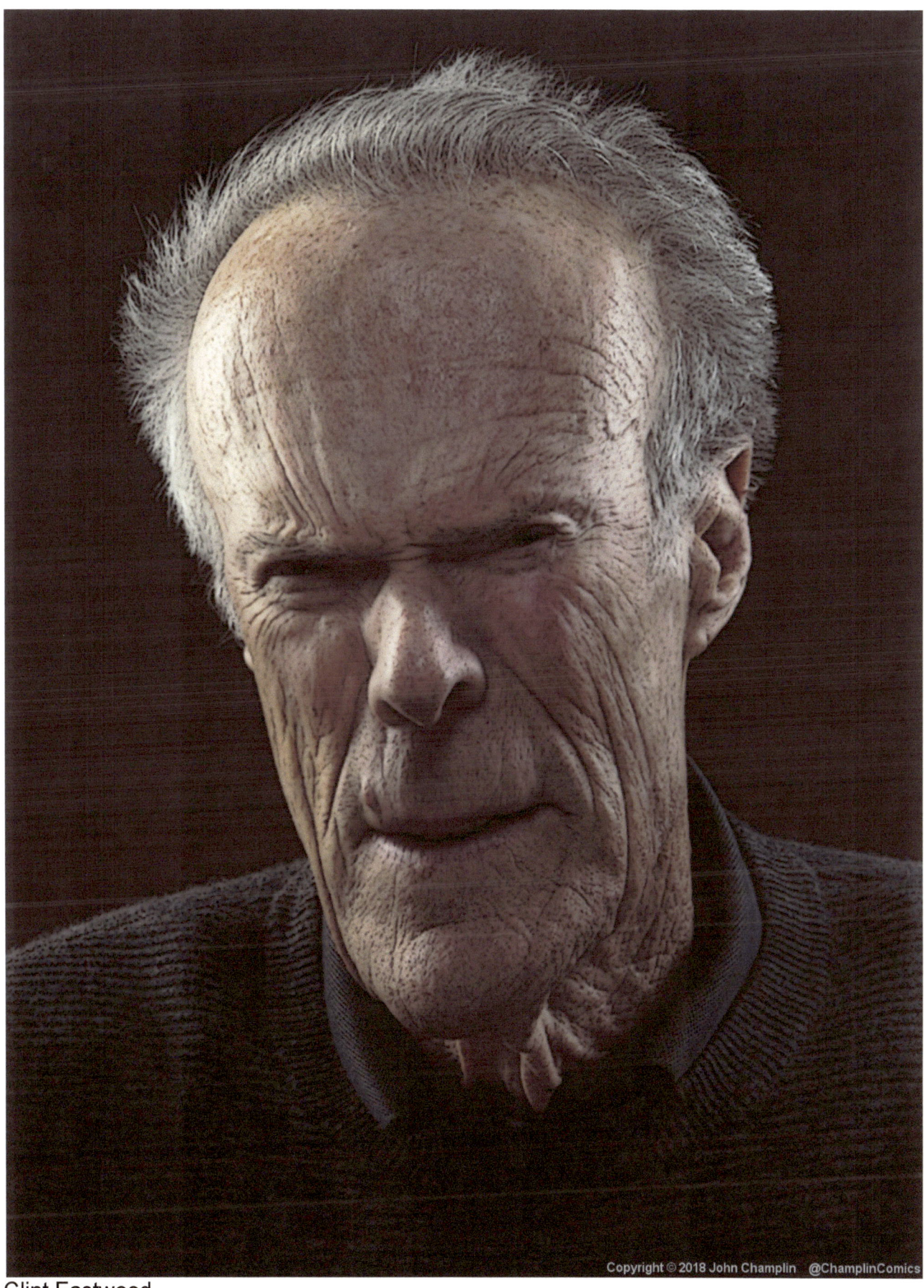

Clint Eastwood

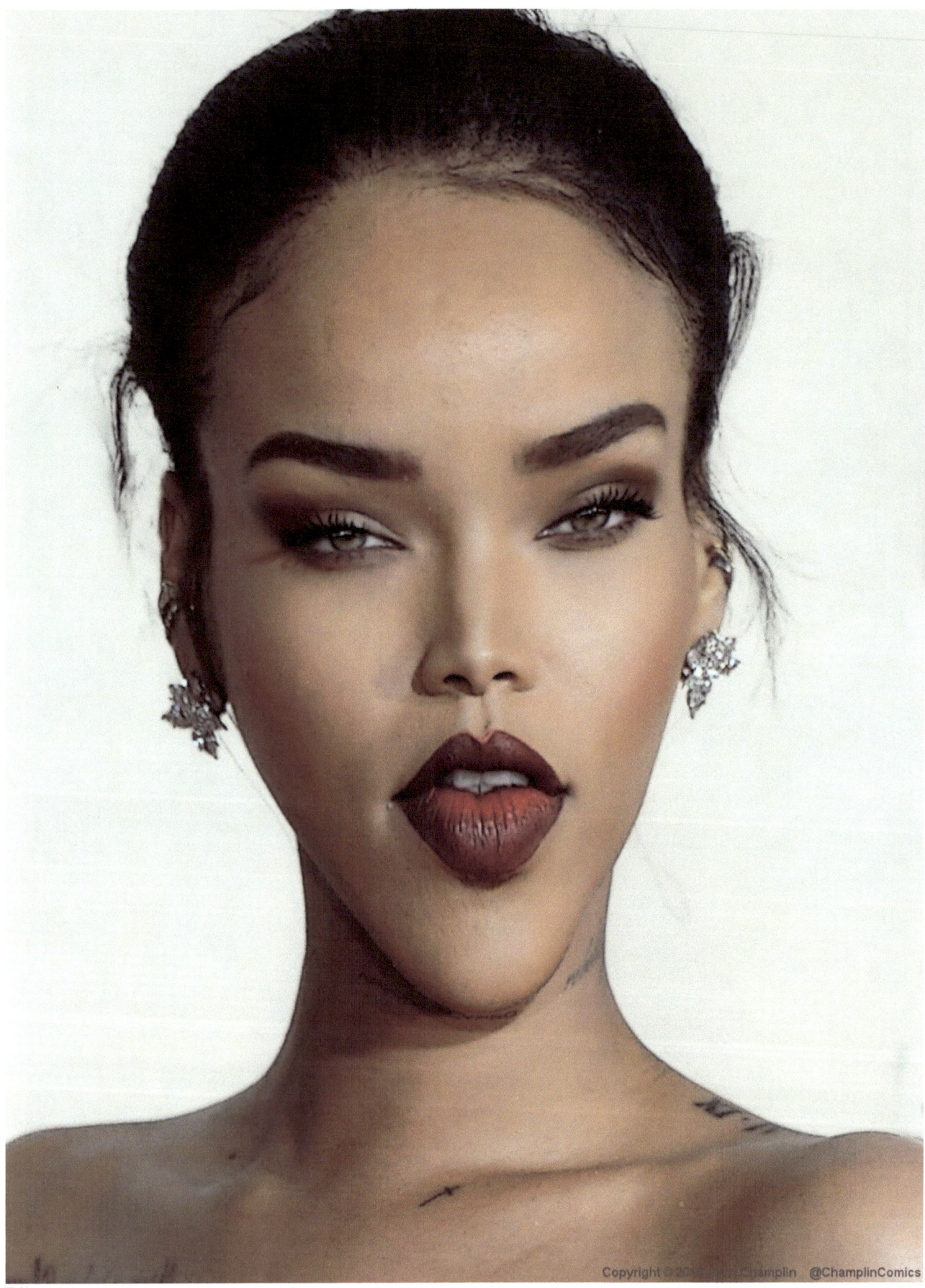

Rihanna

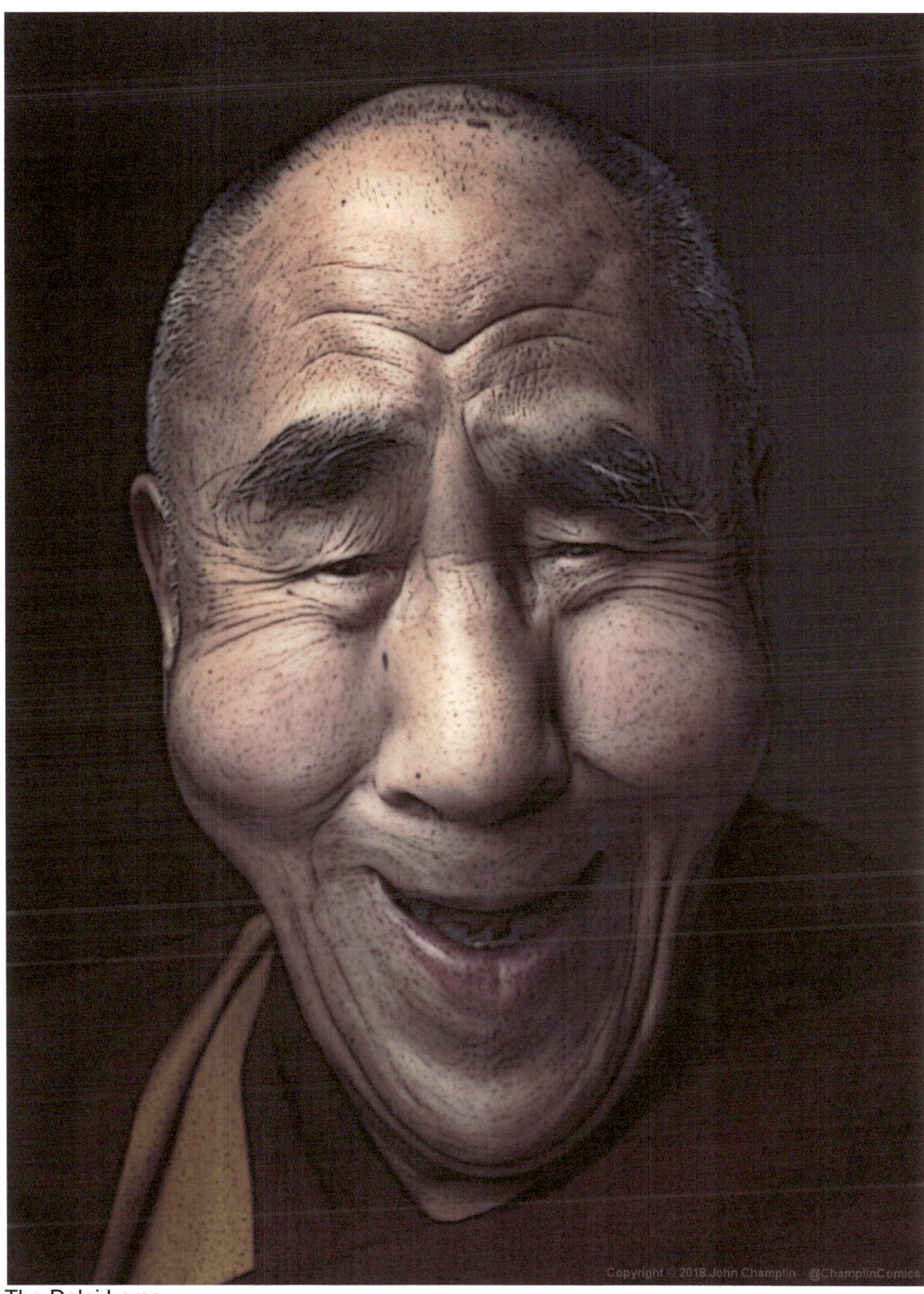

The Dalai Lama

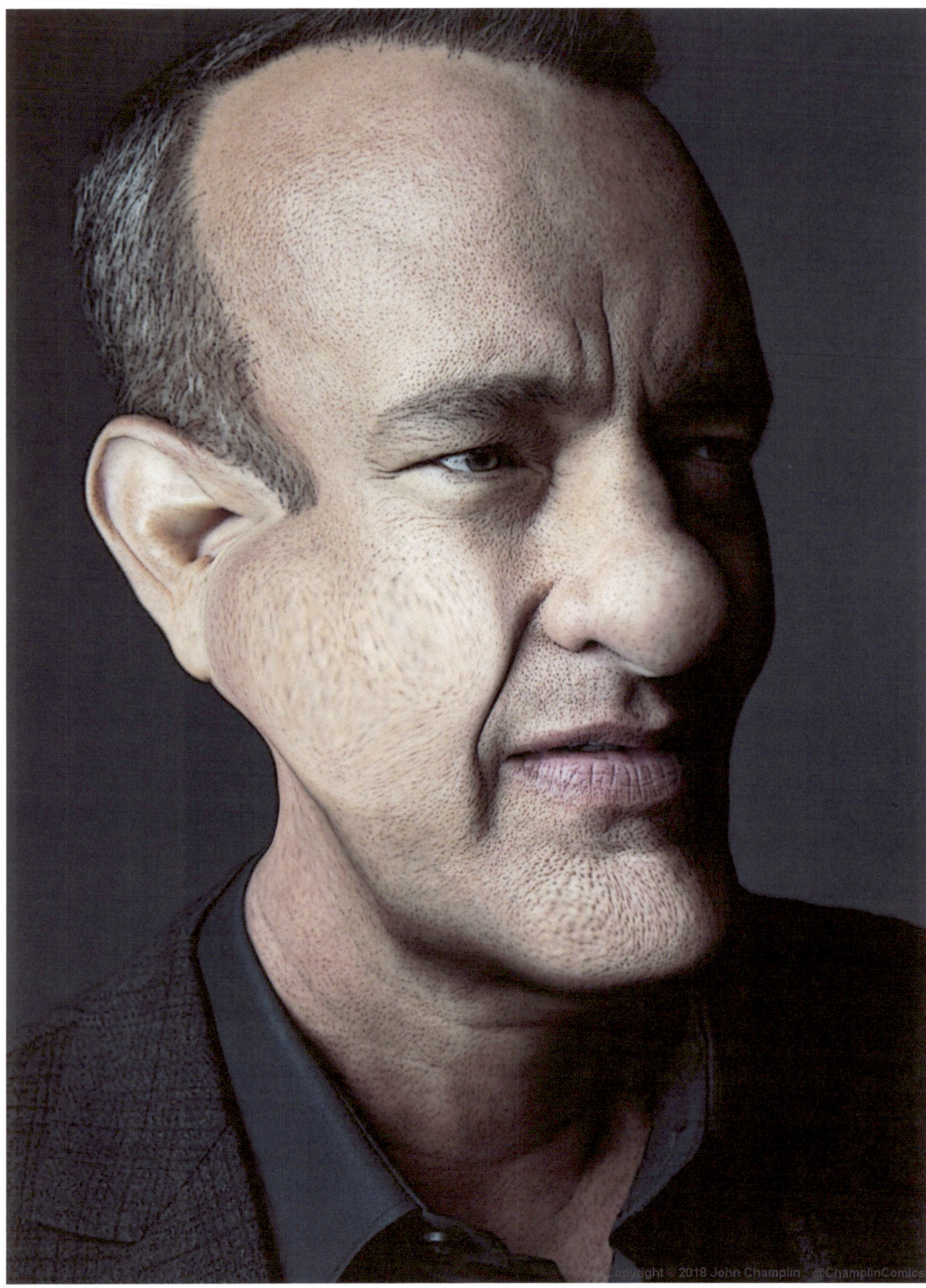

Tom Hanks

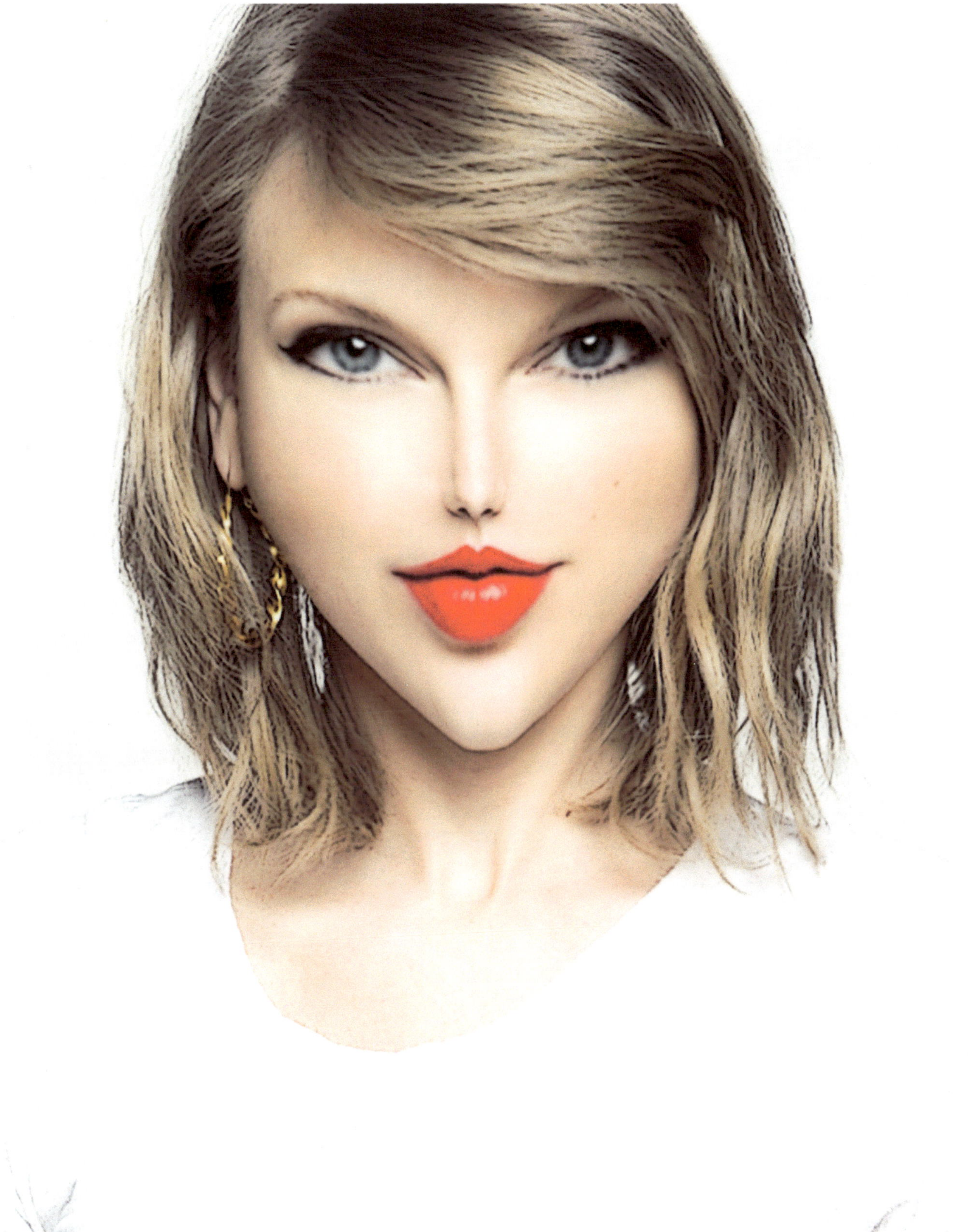

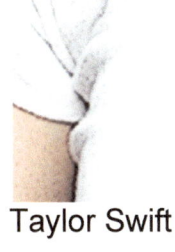

Taylor Swift

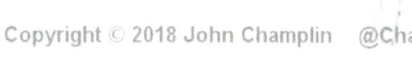

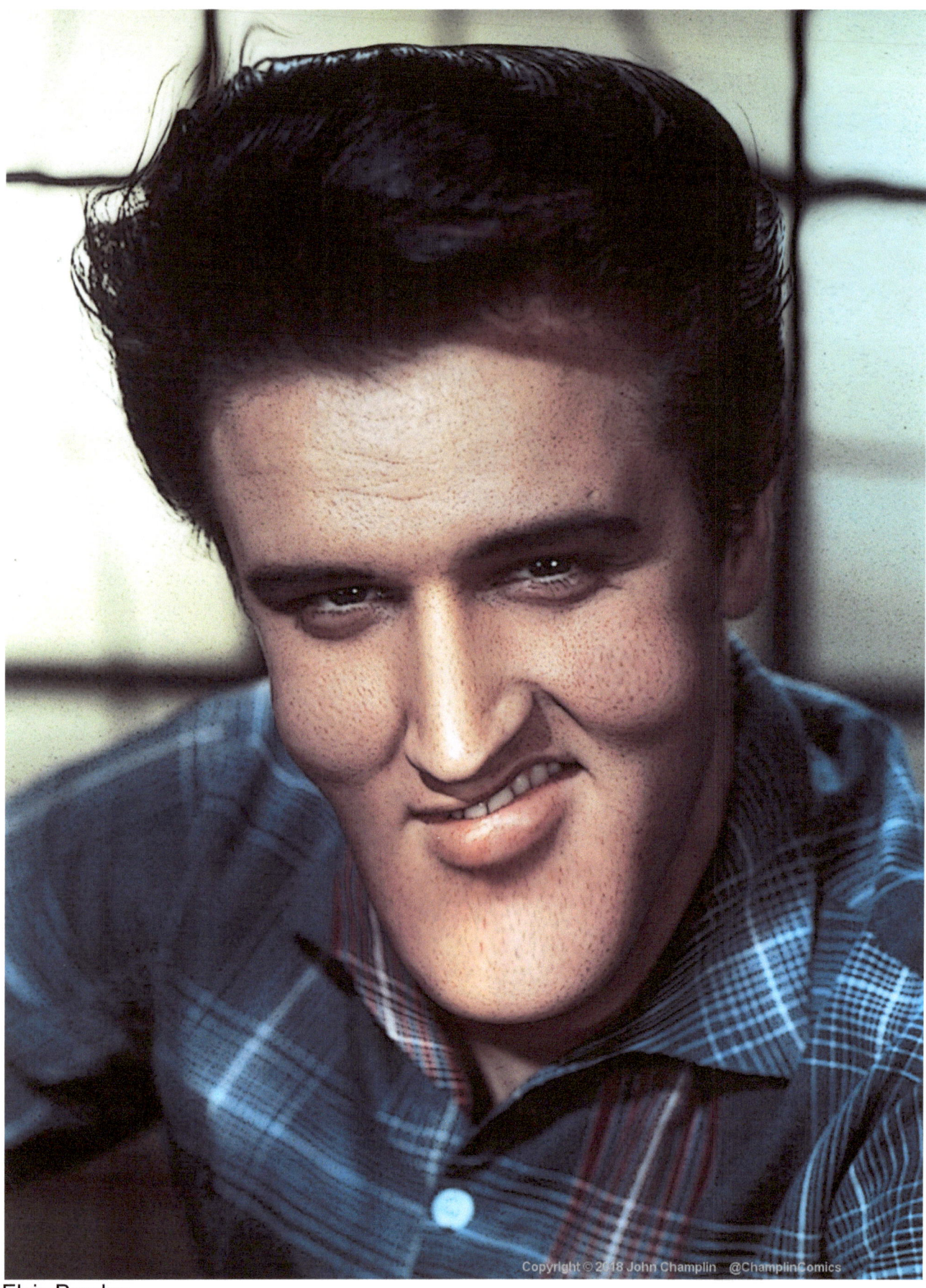

Elvis Presley

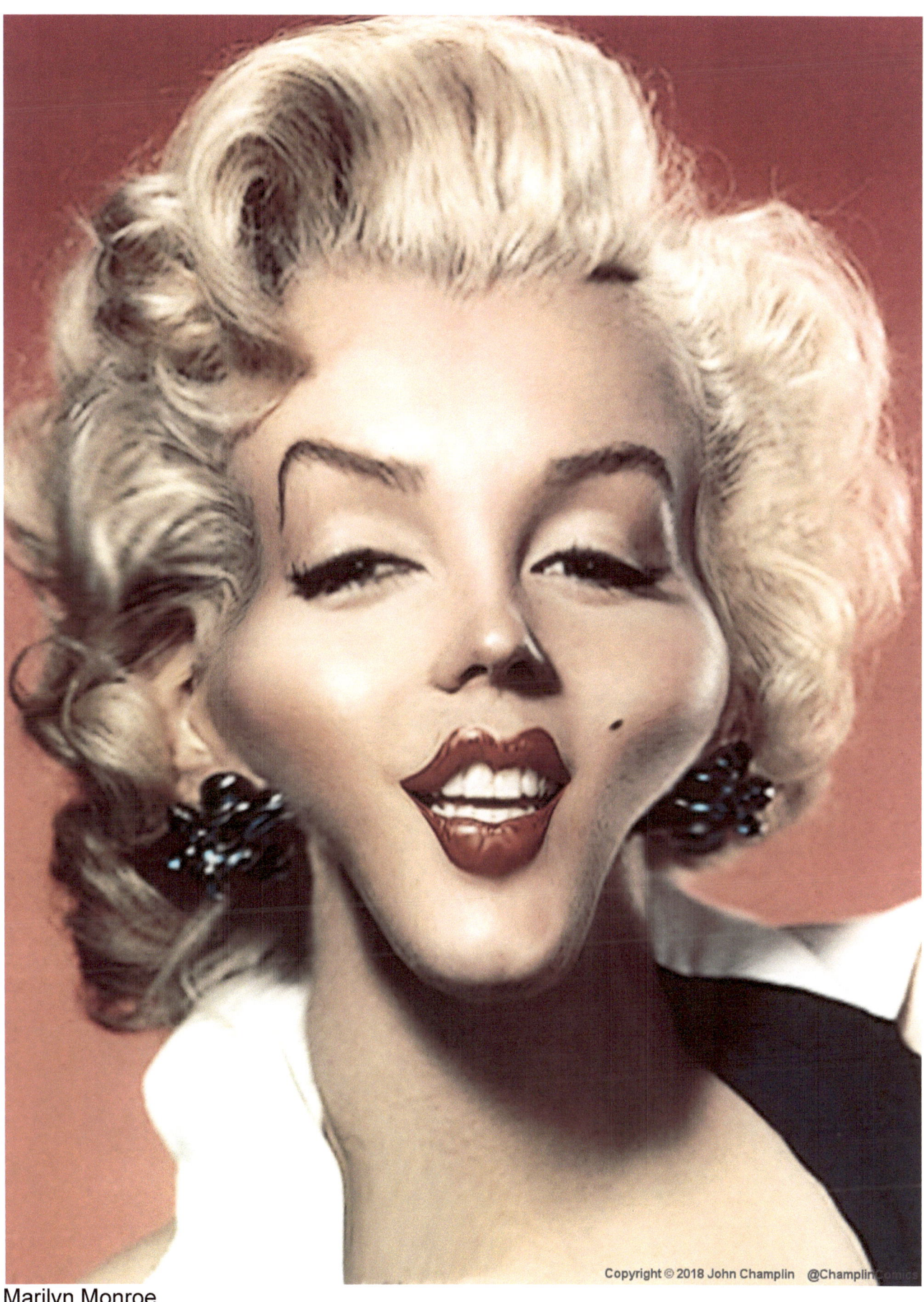

Marilyn Monroe

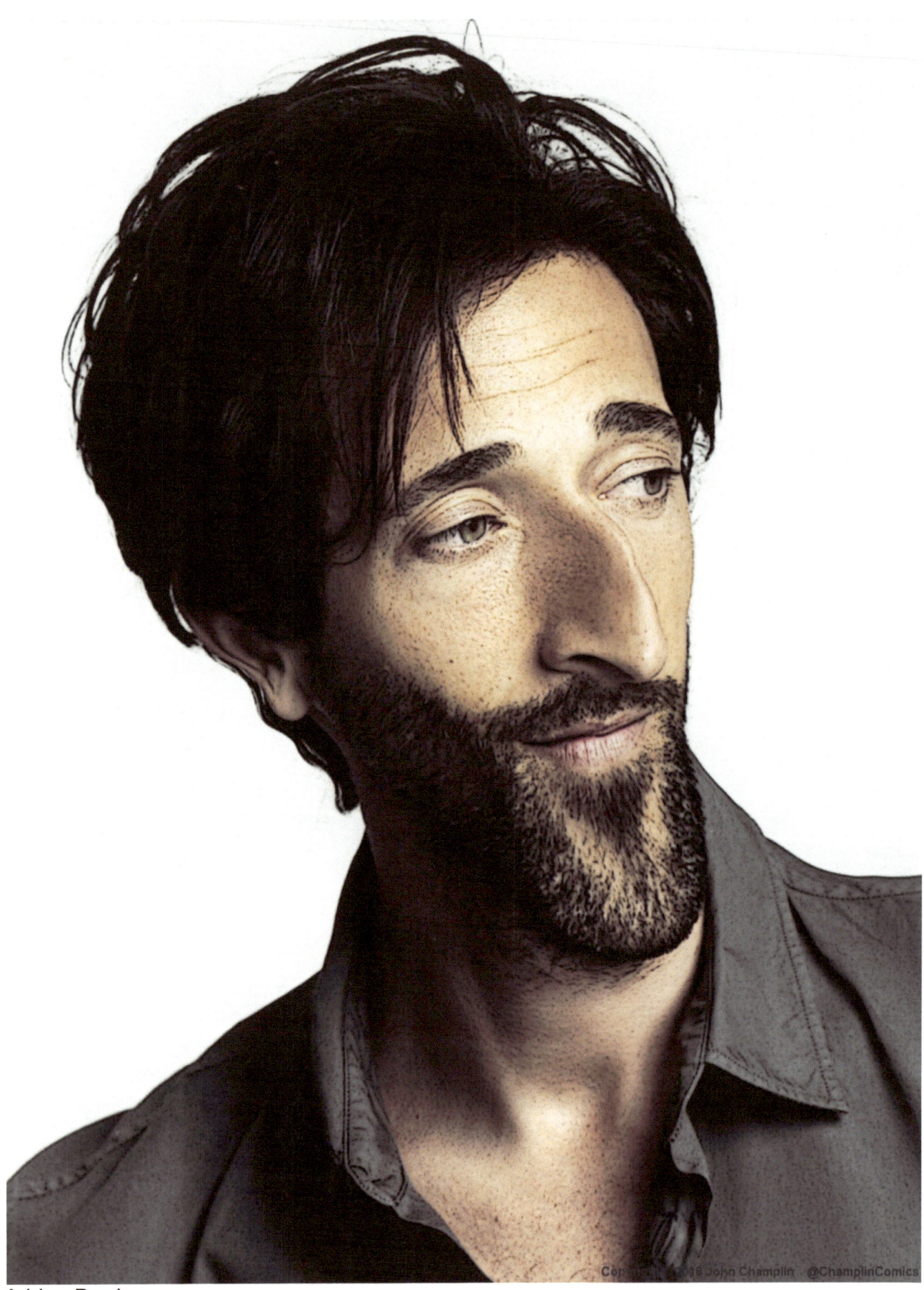

Adrien Brody

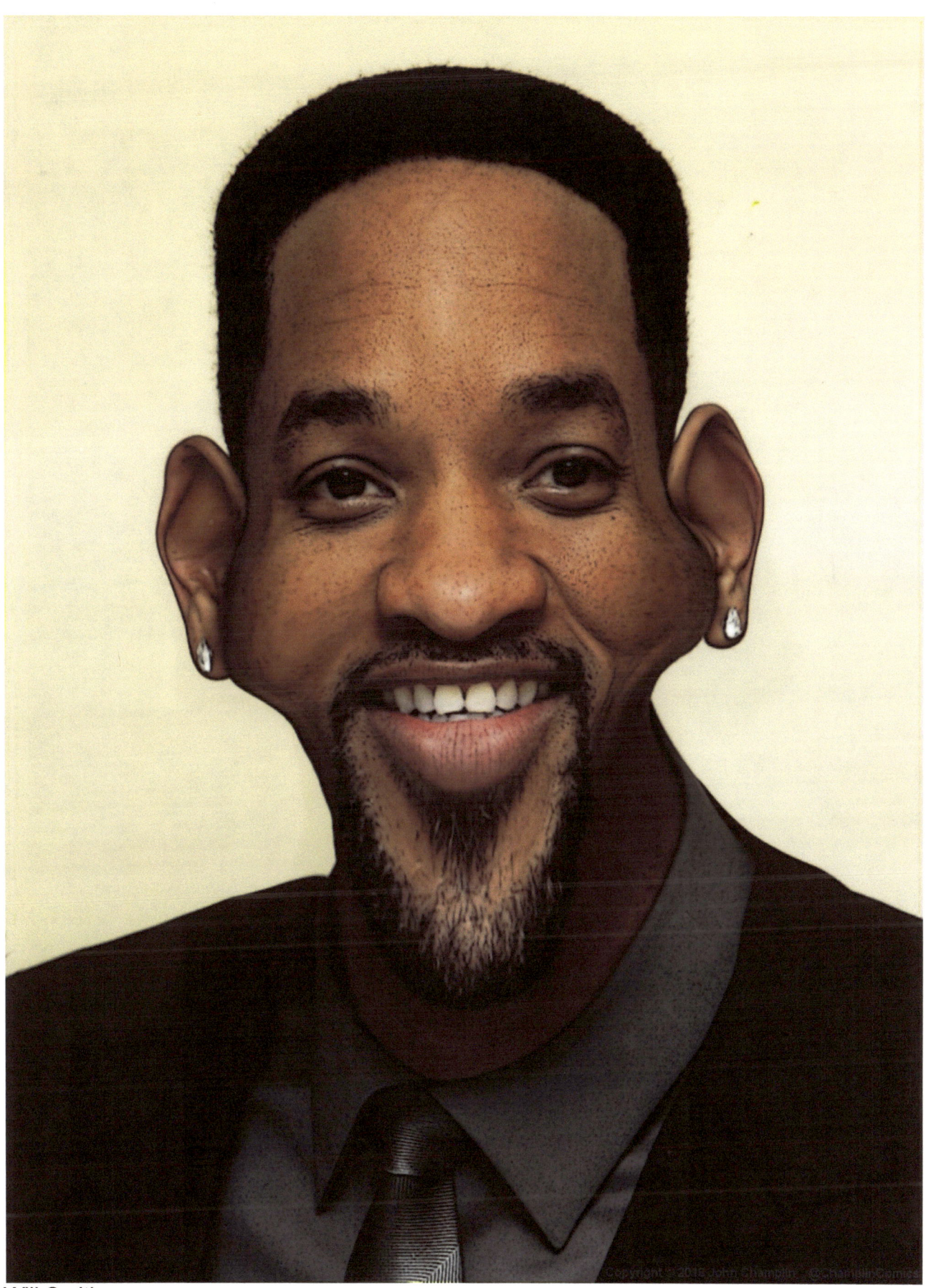

Will Smith

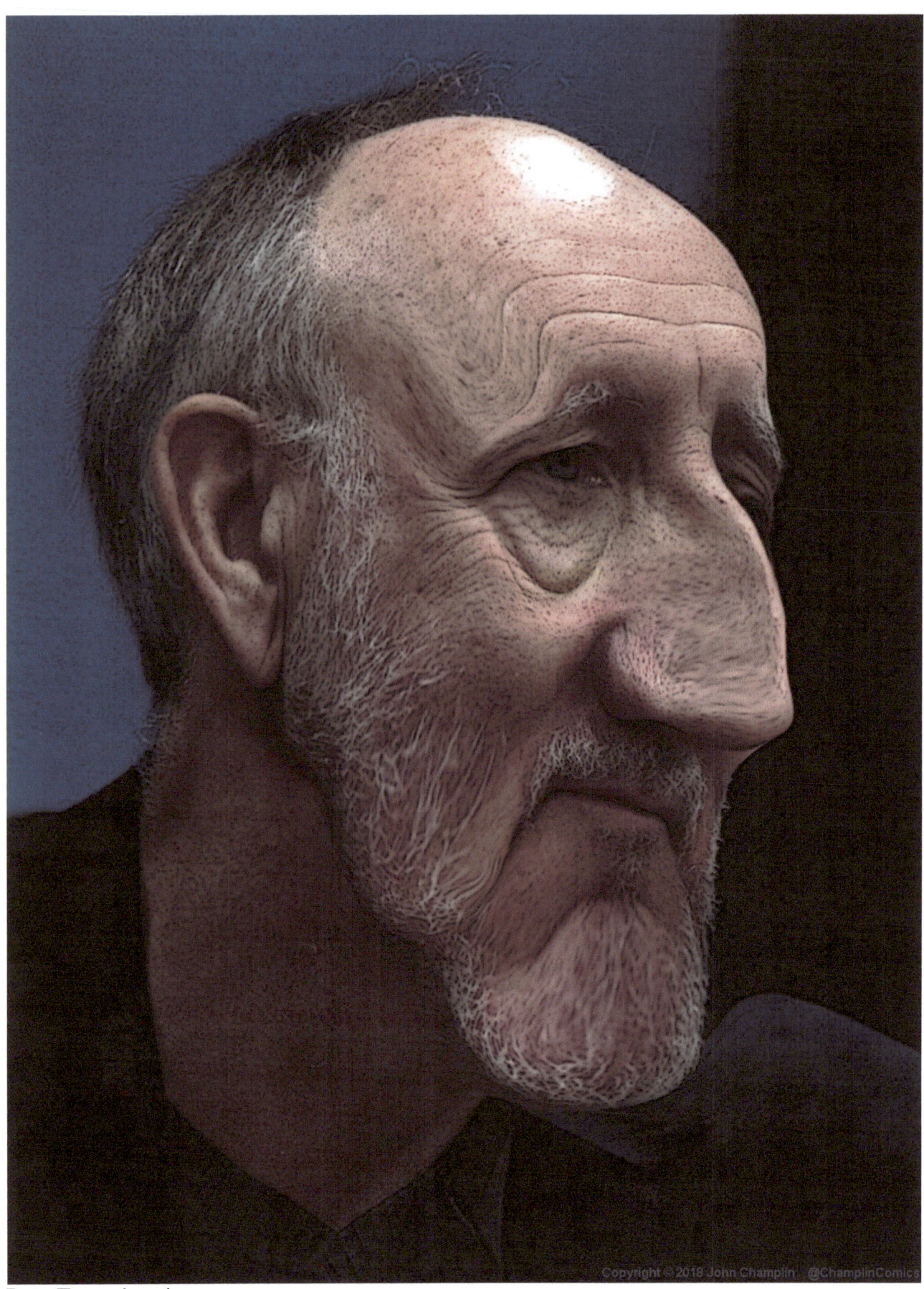

Pete Townshend

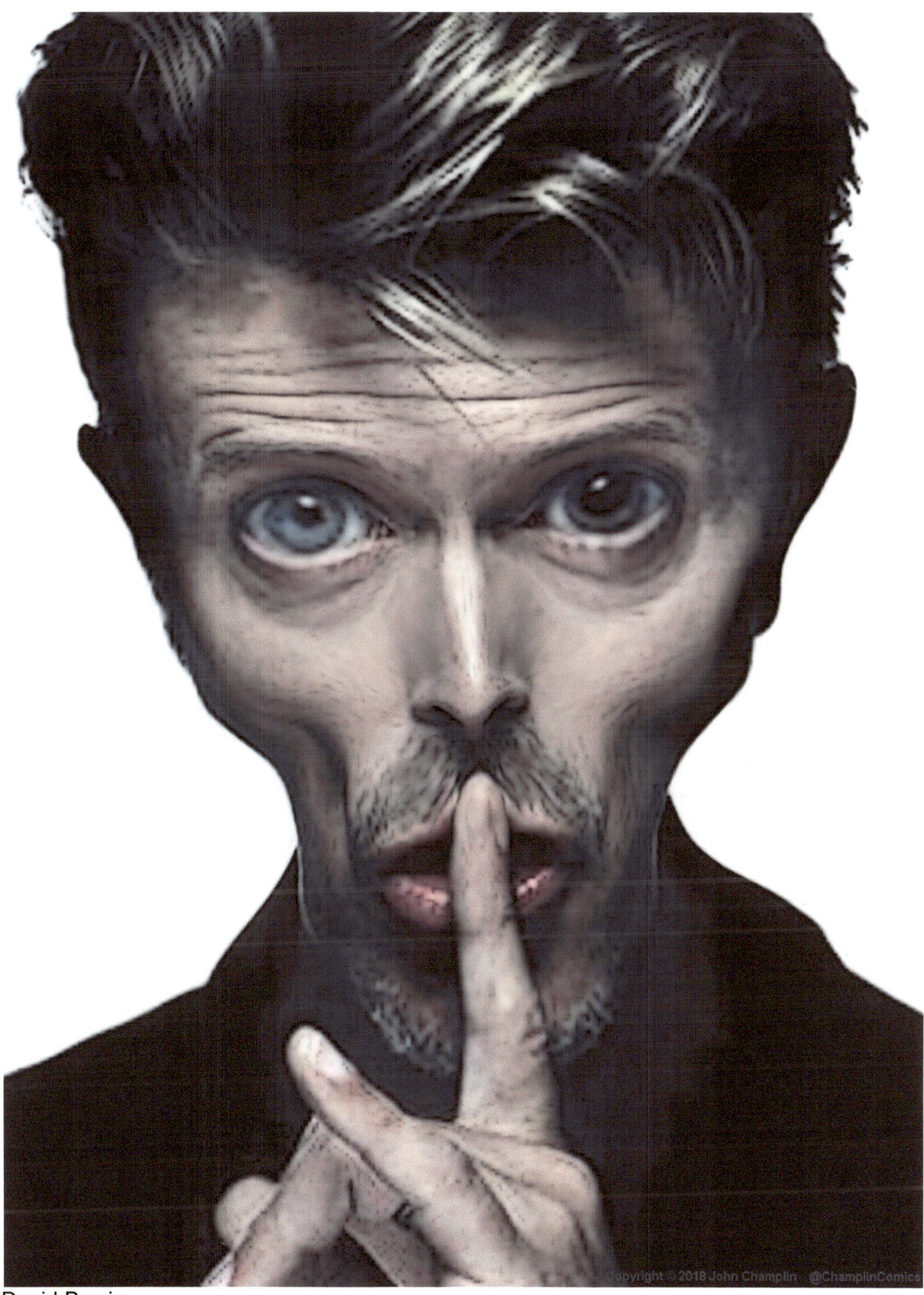

David Bowie

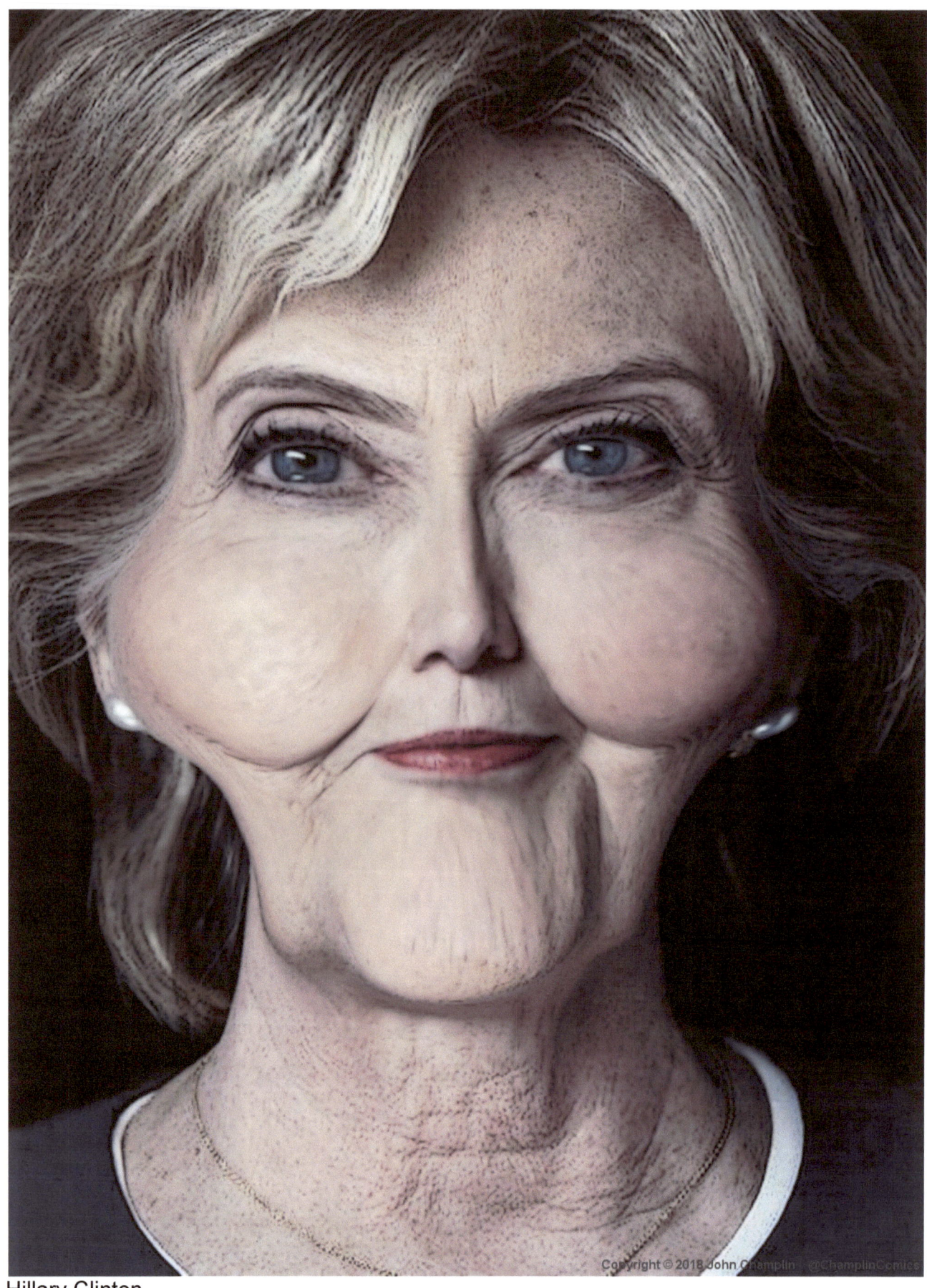

Hillary Clinton

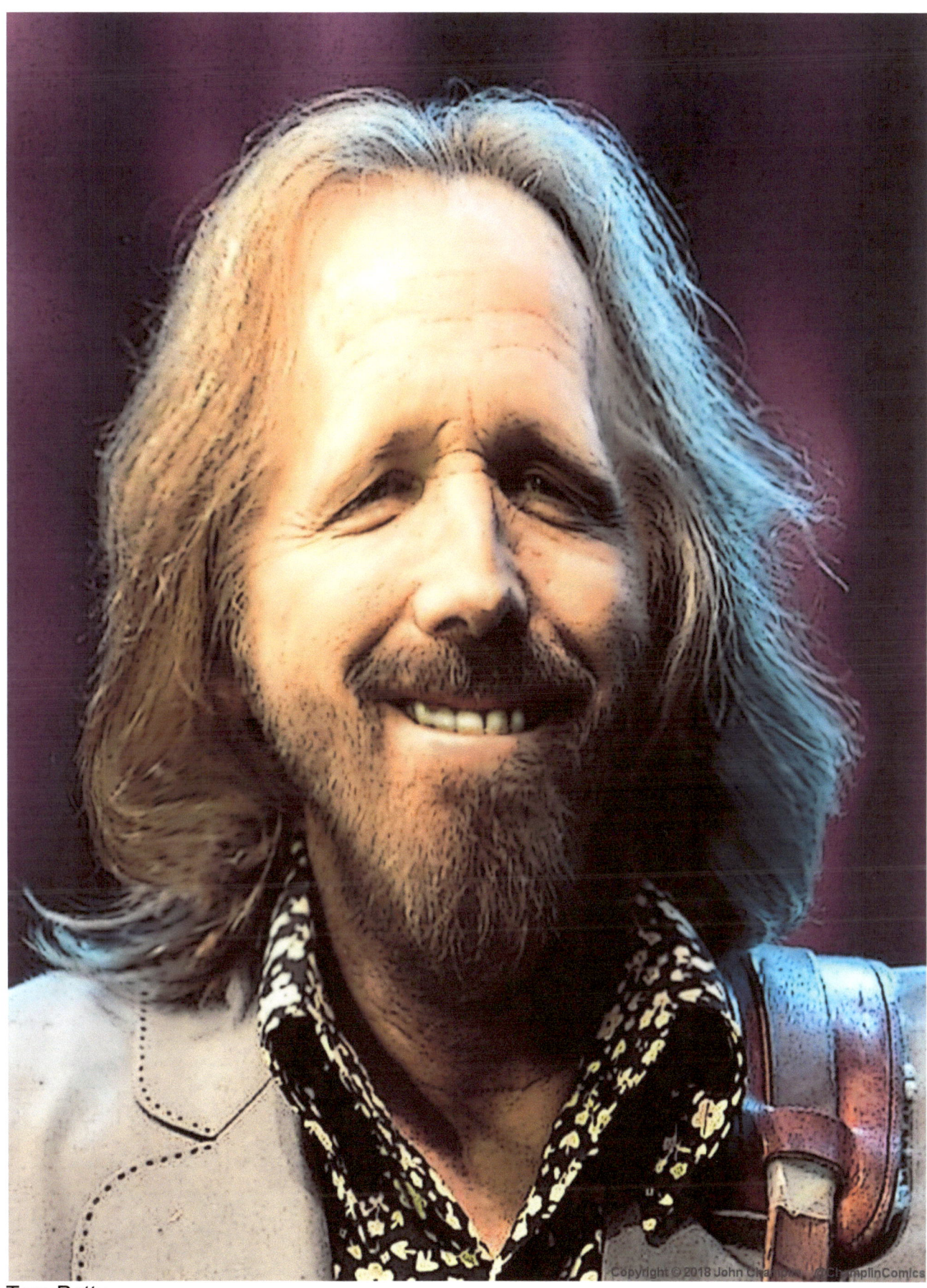

Tom Petty

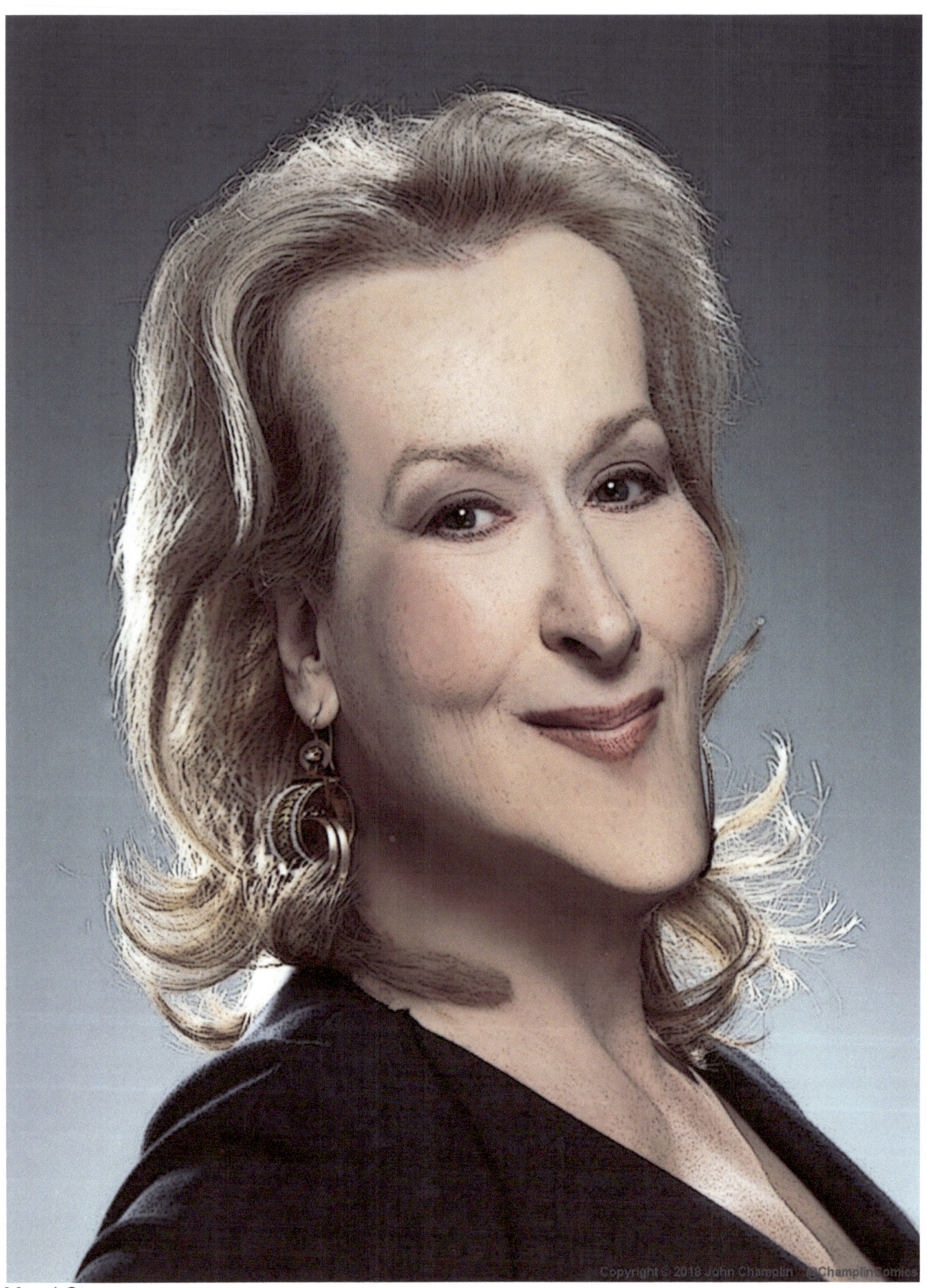

Meryl Streep

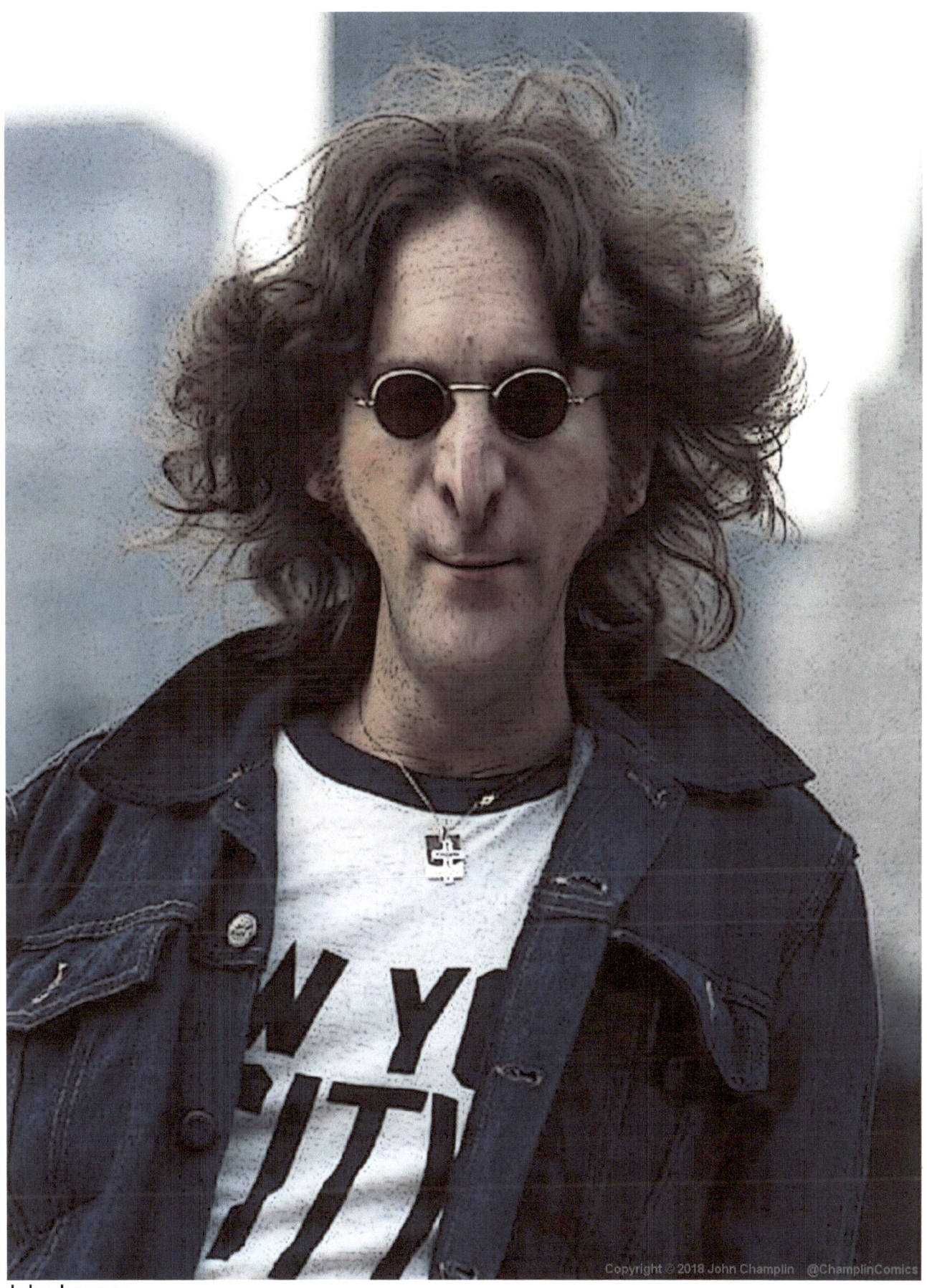

John Lennon

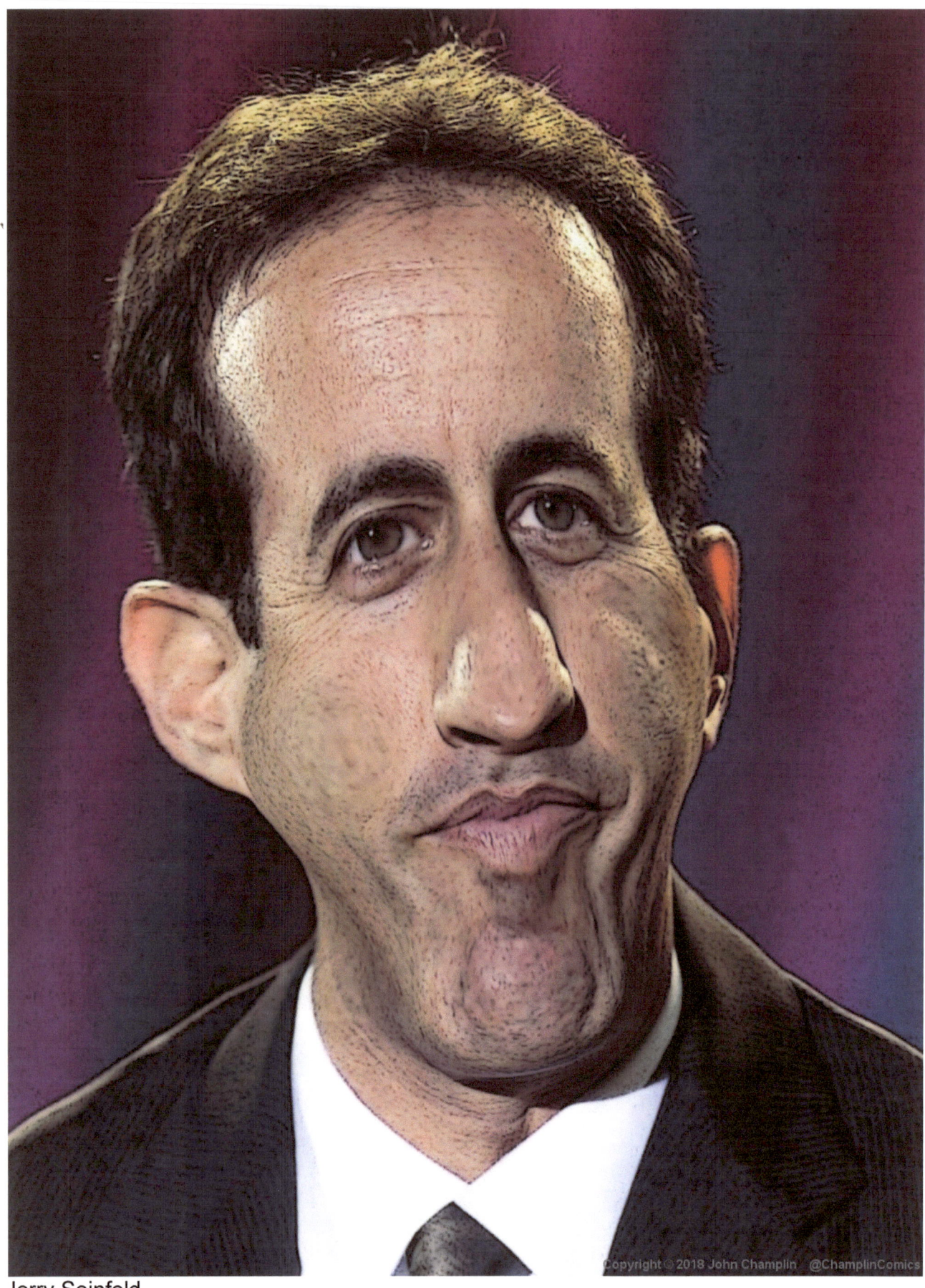

Jerry Seinfeld

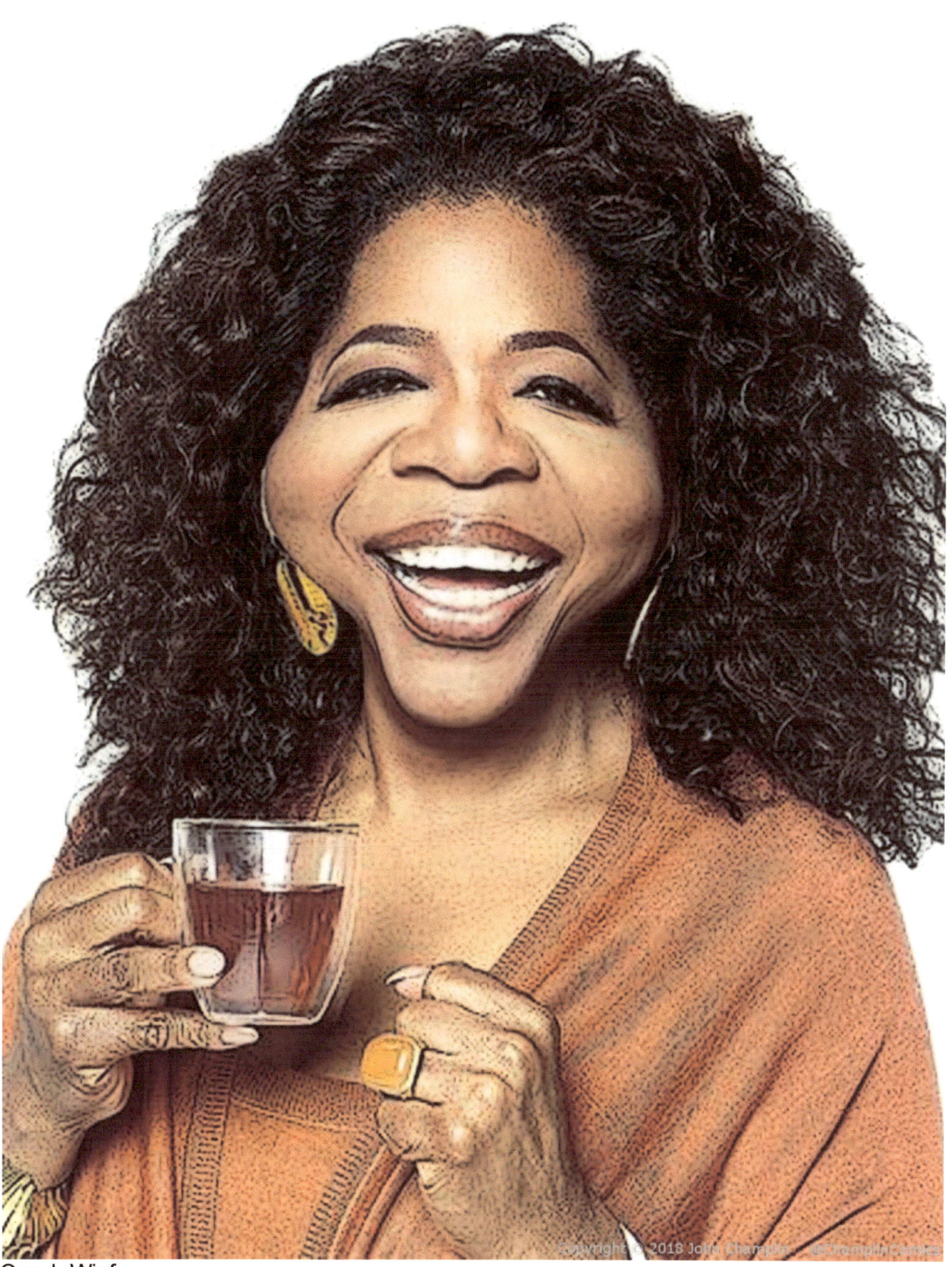

Oprah Winfrey

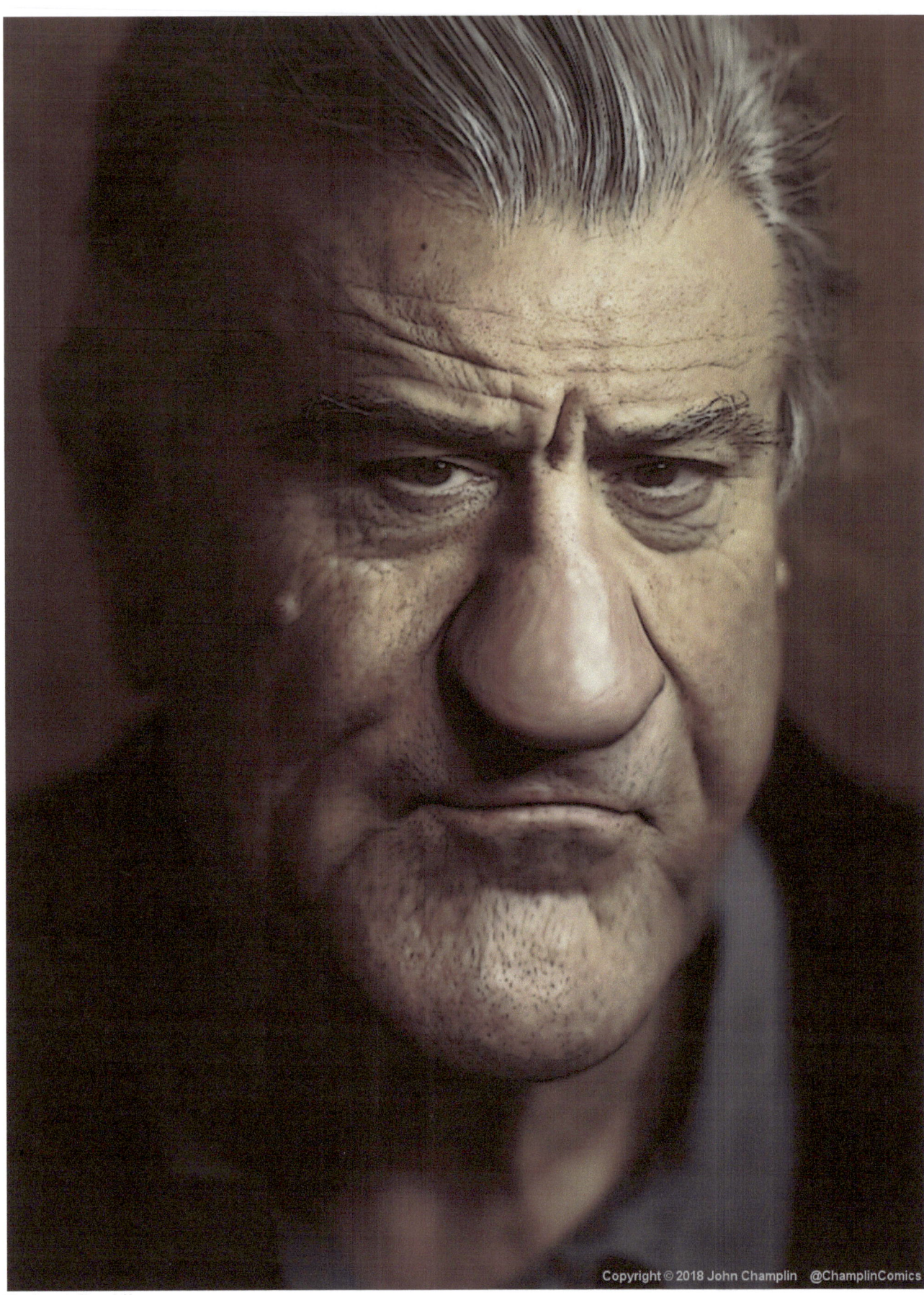

Robert De Niro

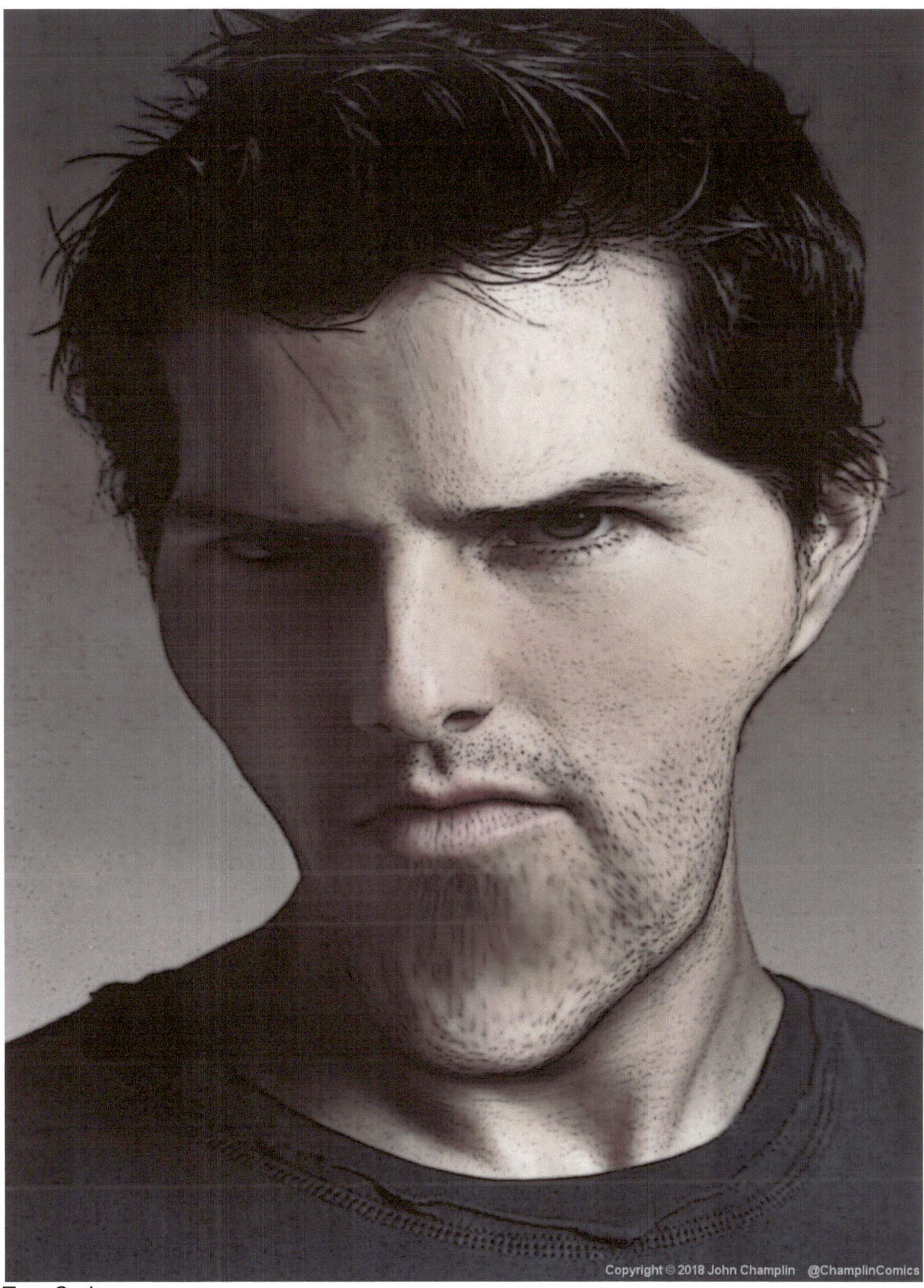

Tom Cruise

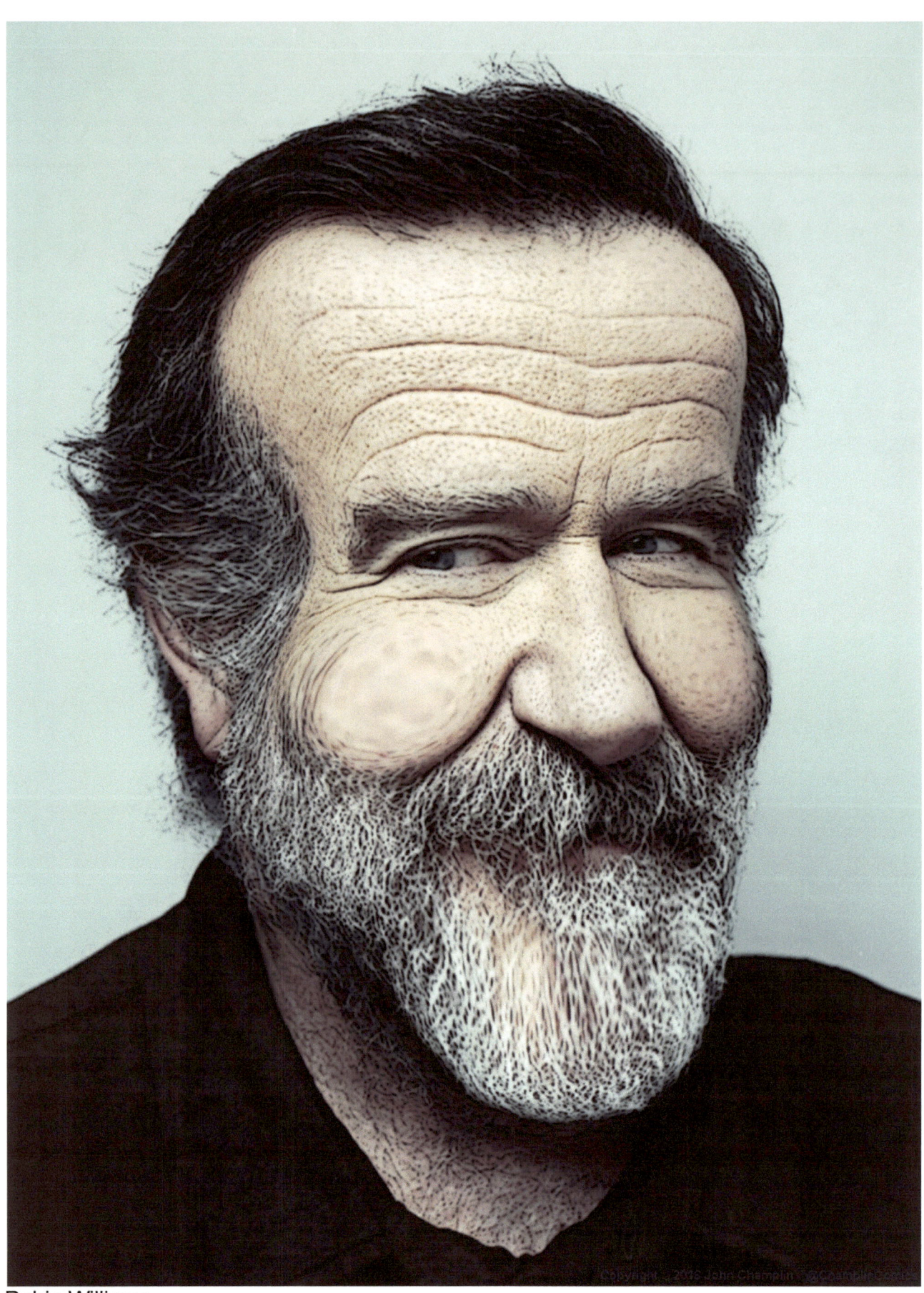

Robin Williams

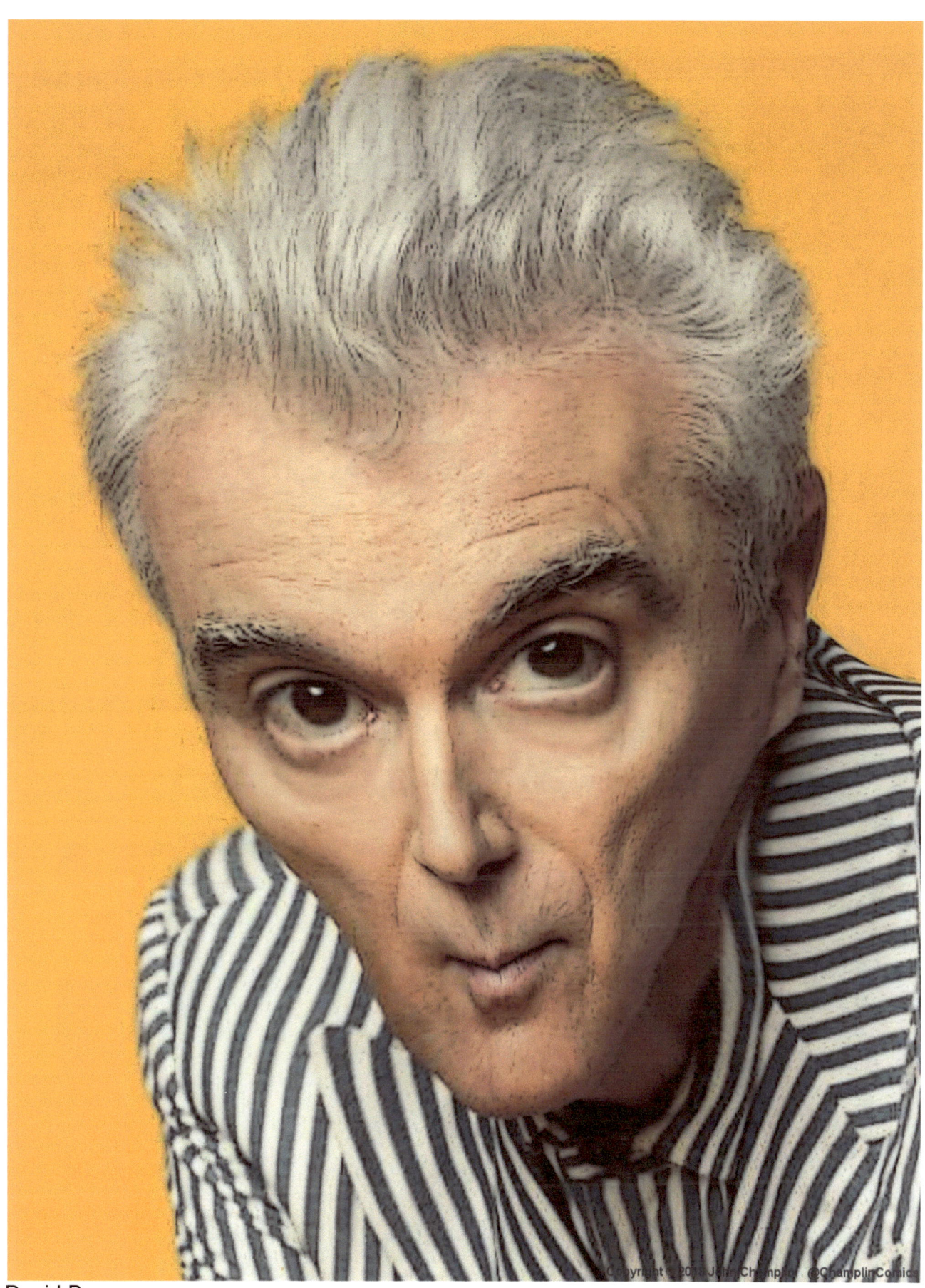
David Byrne

More from @ChamplinComics

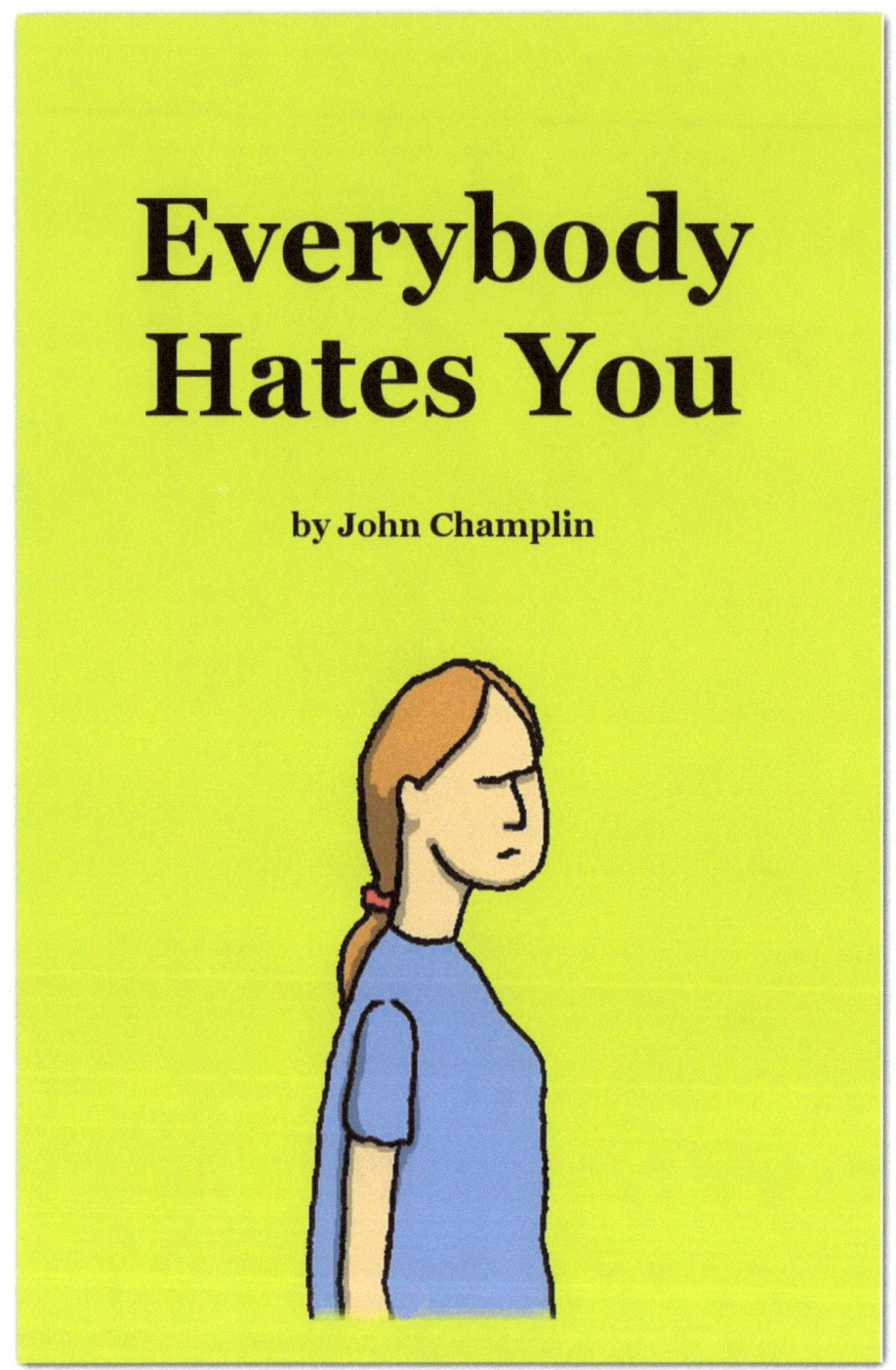

"A sarcastic masterpiece." - Roger 74, Amazon.com

"It will have you rolling beginning to end." - Tyler, Amazon.com

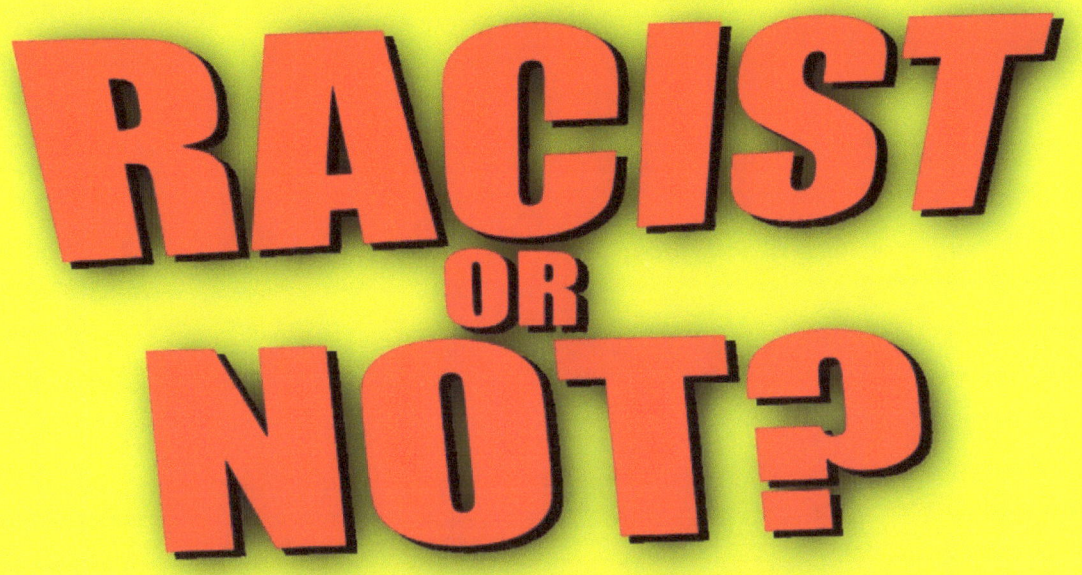

An Adult Coloring Book
You pick the colors. You decide if it's racist or not!

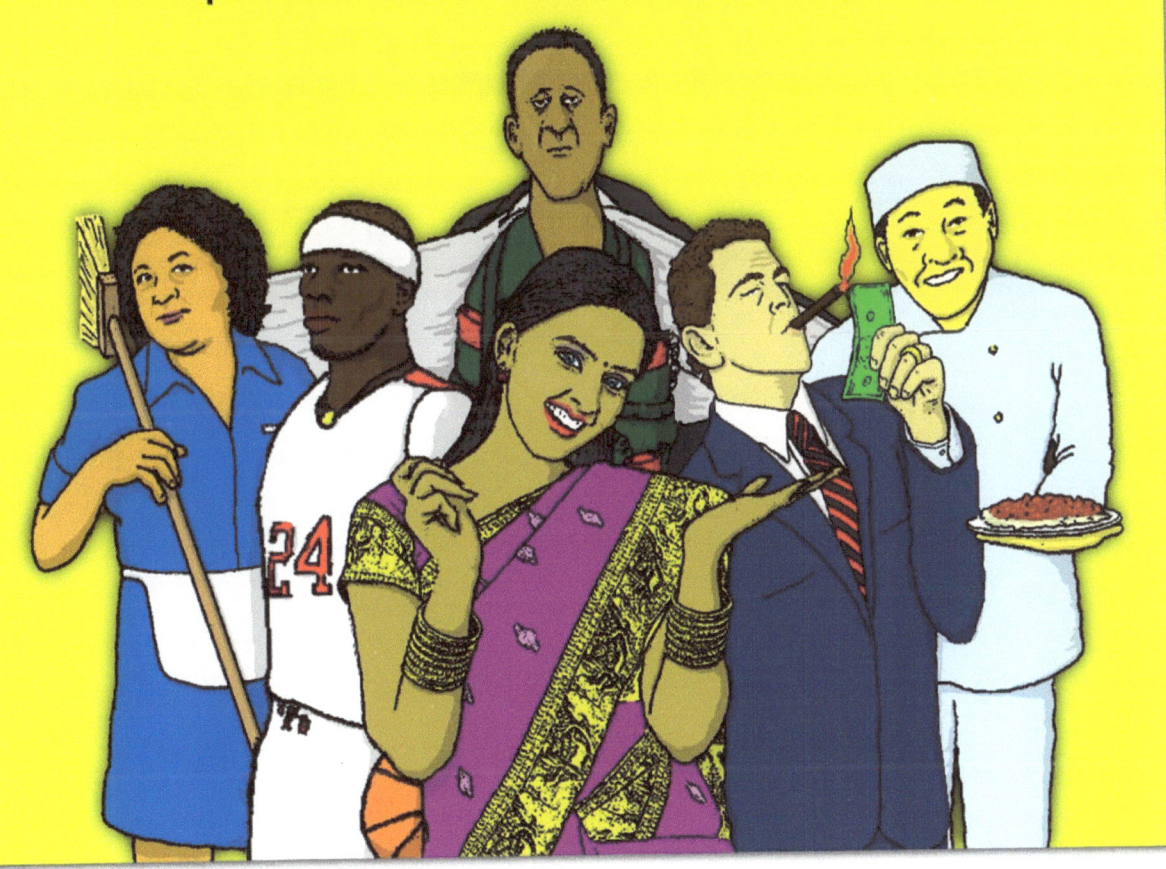

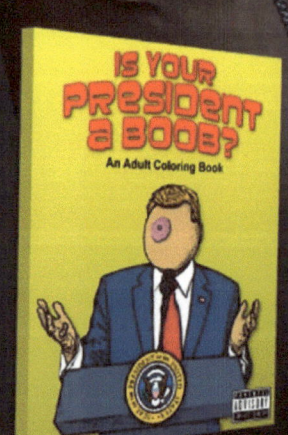

www.ingramcontent.com/pod-product-compliance
Lightning Source LLC
Chambersburg PA
CBHW051214220526
45473CB00003B/1022